Attracting wildlife to your garden

Series Editor:
John Patrick

Rodger Elliot

A LOTHIAN BOOK

Acknowledgements

The enthusiasm and knowledge of gardeners and land-holders who cater for wildlife on their properties has helped to enrich this small publication in many ways. I hope the enthusiasm is catching! There are special thanks to Beryl and Trevor Blake, Paul Thompson, Lyn and John Simpson, Elspeth and Garry Jacobs, Bill Aitchison and Sue Guymer, David Jones, Colin and Liana Joyce, Leanne Weston and Evan Clucas, Glen Wilson, Karwarra Australian Plant Garden in Kalorama, Victoria, and fellow members of 'Iluka'. Ellen McCulloch of the Bird Observers Club of Australia and Stephen Platt from 'Land for Wildlife' provided valuable information.

Also, being a terribly impatient photographer, I was indeed fortunate to be able to include some wonderful shots of birds and animals, taken by friends, Bill and Marion King.

My best mate, Gwen, really warrants the title of co-author but she has graciously declined that offer. I wish she had accepted!

A Lothian Book
Thomas C. Lothian Pty Ltd
11 Munro Street, Port Melbourne
Victoria 3207

Copyright © Rodger Elliot 1994
Copyright © illustrations
Thomas C. Lothian Pty Ltd 1994
First published 1994

National Library of Australia
Cataloguing-in-publication data:

Elliott, W. Rodger, 1941-
    Attracting wildlife to your garden

    Includes index
    ISBN 0 85091 628 3.

    1. Garden fauna — Australia. 2. Gardening to attract wildlife — Australia. 3. Gardening to attract birds — Australia. I. Title.
    (Series: Lothian Australian gardening series).

639.920994

Cover design by David Constable
Illustrations by Julia McLeish
Typeset in Cheltenham and Rockwell by Mackenzies
Printed in Australia by Impact Printing

Foreword

Our efforts to attract wildlife to the suburban environment are succeeding. Most government conservation agencies are now addressing the issue of wildlife corridors to encourage the movement of wildlife and this means that even the most urban-based Australian can see something of our native wildlife.

I know from my own observations of the park next to my home that native animals and birds frequent cities. Lorikeets and parrots are regular visitors, together with silver-eyes and honeyeaters and while we also see exotics, it is the native avifauna that gives my family special pleasure.

As Rodger Elliot points out in this most timely book, there is much we can do as householders to encourage our magnificent wildlife. Although we may never have our backyard full of Leadbeater's Possums, the birds and animals we do attract will not only improve our lifestyle but also reduce our dependence on chemicals by acting as predators on our garden pests. The use of native plants is a significant contribution to the well-being of native birds and fauna but we can also assist by protecting them from predators (especially cats) and providing sites for reproduction. A change of attitude from a tidy mind that demands the removal of large dead trees to one where old trees are retained would be a positive start!

Rodger Elliot's book is not only a useful manual, it is also a cry from the heart of a compassionate man who has achieved much to conserve our wildlife. He speaks with experience.

JOHN PATRICK
Series Editor

Contents

Foreword

Introduction   4

Attracting and retaining wildlife   6

    Plant selection and the wildlife environment; Ponds and pools; Habitat garden plans; Maintenance — beware of wildlife needs

Birds in the Australian garden   11

    Native birds; A natural food supply; Supplementary feeding; Water; Shelter for refuge and nesting sites; Pest control; Plant pollination; Bird problems

Butterflies, moths, other insects and spiders   20

    Butterflies or moths?; Migratory habits; Beauty and variety; Life cycles and ecology; Encouraging butterflies and moths to the garden; Plant pollination; Desirable insects and beetles; Spiders; Earthworms; Crickets and grasshoppers; Cicadas

Mammals, reptiles, amphibians and fish   29

    Mammals; Possums; Koalas; Bandicoots; Echidnas; Bush rats; Native mice; Bats; Lizards; Snakes; Frogs; Fish

Plants for wildlife gardens   37

    Annuals and short-lived plants; Grasses, lilies and other tufting plants; Groundcovers; Climbers; Ferns and fern allies; Palms; Shrubs; Trees

Introduced predators   60

    Cats; Dogs; Foxes

Land for Wildlife   62

Further reading   63

Index   64

Introduction

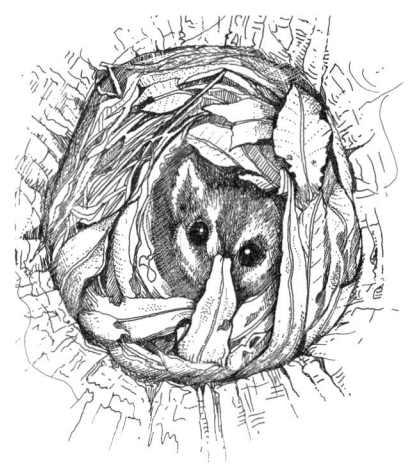

A Sugar Glider nesting in a hollow tree limb.

Australia has an extremely rich, natural heritage. Wildlife has evolved with and, in some cases, is totally dependent on the 25 000 different species of flowering plants. There are 700 different species of Australian native birds; 400 or more butterflies and 20 000 or more moths. Many of these creatures, and others such as lizards (over 250 species), frogs and tortoises, can be encouraged to visit, feed and even breed in our gardens. All of these creatures add a considerable dimension of interest and beauty to the area. They can help to enrich our lives as we enjoy their activities and learn more about their needs and the integral part they play in the web of life.

There has always been a great interest in the native birds of Australia. This is readily understandable — consider their beauty and diversity! Much interest is generated by organisations such as the Bird Observers Club of Australia and the Royal Australasian Ornithologists Union. Both bodies are very active in bird conservation with a range of activities and programmes that cater for differing levels of interest and expertise, for example the fun time of a 'Twitchathon' (an event where competitors spot as many different birds as possible within a set time limit) or the more serious intent of a survey of the flight patterns of the Yellow-tailed Black Cockatoo.

There is nothing quite like being able to sit in a garden and watch the acrobatics of honeyeaters as they gather nectar from flowers. The cacophony that arises from small birds as they announce the arrival of the predatory kookaburra or butcherbird never ceases to amaze me and arouse my interest in their boisterous activities. It is always fascinating to observe the birds which accompany each other in their goings on. On misty and overcast mornings in our previous garden you could nearly always forecast correctly that there would be an influx of Brown Thornbills, Grey Fantails and Eastern Spinebills at the same time. Why? Was it because of the camouflage afforded by dull light? Was it the plentiful availability of insects? Worth pondering! Many birds accept quite freely the presence of humans in the environment, and will sit or feed at close proximity without concern.

Parrots, lorikeets, cockatoos and their relatives are abundant in Australia, with around 55 different species. They range in colour from black, white or grey, through pastel shades to vivid combinations of red, blue, green and yellow. Here is a group of birds which we in Australia should not take for granted because we have one of the richest representations of this spectacular bird group in the world.

Seed-eating birds such as finches, wrens and robins are well represented in Australia, and again these delightful creatures can be encouraged to feel quite at home if suitable conditions are established in our gardens. Larger seed-eaters such as pigeons and members of the parrot family can be regular visitors where appropriate food plants grow. Some of the other widespread species such as magpies, kookaburras and members of the owl family can only be expected to reside where there are areas of mature trees to provide shelter and nesting sites.

Other marvellous and captivating wildlife, such as the invertebrates which make up 90 per cent of our animal life, are sure to be present in our gardens for varying periods of time. Some are never given much prominence, except perhaps for butterflies. Enthusiasts have been interested in the butterflies of Australia for many years, but it is only recently, as growers of Australian plants began to appreciate the value of butterfly-attracting plants, that there has been more widespread interest in this particular group of beautiful and charming insects. Undoubtedly developments such as the butterfly houses at Kuranda in Queensland, the Royal Melbourne Zoo in Victoria and in other places have added to this enthusiasm as has, to some extent, the interest in cottage-style gardening and the growing of plants such as everlasting daisies, which seem to bring butterflies from almost nowhere on a warm, sunny day.

Many keen Australian plant gardeners were attracted to gardening initially by a desire to encourage native birds into their home environments. This book is about helping to make this possible and also, importantly, expanding the range of wildlife that can be attracted and retained in the garden. If you have an established garden, or perhaps you are just planning to start one in the 'suburban desert' of a new subdivision; this book will show you how to create a haven for wildlife.

Australian native plants, animals, birds and insects are part of a natural pattern that is intricately woven. The term used to describe this situation is 'ecology'. Ecology is derived from the Greek word *oikos*, meaning a house or dwelling place. The Oxford Dictionary of Natural History defines ecology as the 'scientific study of the interrelationships among organisms and between organisms, and all aspects, living and non-living of their environment'. Ecology is the cornerstone and the key to building a habitat for wildlife in our gardens.

Our observations, actions and experiences can help make our endeavours successful. We can play a valuable and enjoyable part in fostering this fascinating interdependence by providing suitable habitats. This will not only enable us to enjoy the wildlife but we will also have the opportunity to learn more about the complex ecological system in our garden. We might see ants curating the caterpillars and pupae of the Common Imperial Blue butterflies on young *Acacia dealbata* or *Acacia mearnsii* plants — the educational benefits and inspiration for us and visitors to our gardens are immense.

How wonderful it would be if neighbours could create corridors of valuable wildlife habitat which in time would link up with native bushland. This would be of immeasurable value to the animals and our enjoyment of their presence would be a marvellous reward. Wouldn't it be lovely to have regular visits by bandicoots and wallabies! Some fortunate gardeners beyond the bounds of suburbia do. We may even be able to aid the conservation of some rare or endangered species!

Every wildlife gardener is an ecologist!

Attracting and retaining wildlife

If we wish to attract wildlife to our garden we must provide a suitable habitat or 'living place' for communities of plants and animals. A habitat for native wildlife comprises three very important elements:
- Shelter — a refuge for resting, nesting or residence
- Food — available, if possible, all year round
- Water — the presence of permanent water.

Planting and nurturing suitable grasses, lilies, waterplants, groundcovers, shrubs and trees will provide sanctuary and shelter for wildlife as well as making food available.

Plant selection and the wildlife environment

In nature there is always a greater concentration of wildlife where different plant communities merge or overlap, such as where rainforest and woodland, or heathland and woodland meet. In some cases, three or four plant communities will converge. This aspect is well worth incorporating in our efforts to create a habitat for animals, birds and insects. The wildlife you attract may pay regular visits and, hopefully, some will become residents and breed in your garden. To provide a suitable wildlife habitat a diversity of plants must be top priority. Diversity is strength, as provision is made to cater for a wide range of wildlife. Limitation of the palette of plants will decrease the likelihood of attracting large numbers of creatures.

Birds and animals are more likely to visit and/or nest in wild and even somewhat unkempt areas of vegetation. Rarely do rigidly manicured gardens provide the conditions that appeal to a wide diversity of birds and animals. Gardens that have a regimented appearance, with nothing ever out of place — closely mown lawns, clipped shrubs and areas that are regularly doused with pesticides and herbicides — may only be visited by some of the more sedentary birds such as magpies, introduced blackbirds, indian mynahs and sparrows. Unless there are trees, shrubs, groundcovers, grasses and lilies with nooks, crevices and curled leaves in which insects and other small animals can live or hide as well as a marvellous mulch of twigs and leaves covering the soil, your chances of attracting wildlife will be severely reduced.

Organic mulch is prized by many gardeners for its moisture-conserving properties and it is an essential component for wildlife gardens. Not only will mulch be the home of insect larvae — a food source for a number of animals — it also is important for small animals, such as lizards, as a place to hibernate during winter. If the mulch is moist from winter through summer to early autumn lizards may deposit their eggs there for safe hatching. What delight!

A pool in your garden will be a wildlife drawcard. (DESIGN: EVAN CLUCAS)

Preferred habitats

Crested Shrike-tits, lorikeets, rufous and Golden Whistlers have a preference for tall trees. Olive-backed Orioles which migrate to southern Australia in spring and summer prefer to nest in bushland, although they have been recorded as nesting in gardens which have dense vegetation.

Often a pile of dead branches which has a climber or creeper entwined is the perfect habitat for some of the small birds such as wrens, thornbills and the Red-browed Firetail Finch. Clumps of unmown grass are favoured by caterpillars as well as small frogs, especially if there are a few hollows where water gathers during and after rain.

In planning a garden for wildlife it is worth considering a range of plants with different heights, so that there are some areas of dense vegetation with tussocks, groundcovers, small to tall shrubs and trees and some open, grassy spots. This will allow the birds and animals a greater choice in selecting suitable sites for refuge and hopefully long-term residence.

Ponds and pools

Creating a permanent pond or pool has possibly the greatest impact on attracting and retaining wildlife in a garden. A well-designed and constructed pool suitably planted for wildlife can give enjoyment beyond description. Within a very short time of the pool filling with water, insects of all types and sizes will find the water magnetic. Birds will come to bathe and drink on its edges. If the pool is large enough birds may be seen aquaplaning for short distances, like rookie aeroplane pilots learning landing procedures. Apart from what seems their obvious enjoyment, birds use this activity to flush out their feathers.

What about mosquitoes? This is one of the first questions asked by most people who contemplate putting in a pool. The answer is fairly simple — frogs and fish — they are highly efficient mosquito-eaters. I recommend that both poolside vegetation and waterplants be established for about six months before introducing fish to a pool. This allows the plants to develop to the stage where there will be ample coverage to provide a protected habitat for the fish and/or frogs.

An ideal pool

Much enjoyment is to be gained from a simple, shallow, reflective pool. Of course, a pool for wildlife may lose that tranquillity for most of the day but there will be times of serenity when ravishing designs of plants, birds and animals will be mirrored on the surface, or you can sit back and watch the ripples caused by frogs, fish or other water-dwellers. On still, overcast days wildlife activity is usually quite frantic around a pool and it can become a focal point.

For those who are fortunate to have potter's-clay subsoil it should be possible to construct a wonderful pool. For other areas where the soils drain like a kitchen colander there are many malleable materials suitable for use as long-lasting pool-liners. Alternative construction materials are acceptable but for an ecologically sustainable pool it is desirable to line the pool base with a jacket of soil before filling it with water. For detailed information on pool construction, see *Water In Your Garden* by Paul Thompson, in the Lothian Australian Garden Series. This publication provides many tips and much

Plants suited to partial submersion

Code for plant groups

f = fern
tu = tussock or clump-forming plants
g = groundcover
ss = small shrub
ts = tall shrub
t = tree

Baumea articulata	tu
Blechnum minus	f
B. nudum	f
Carex fascicularis	tu
C. gaudichaudiana	tu
Chorizandra enodis	tu
Crassula helmsii	g
Gleichenia dicarpa	f
G. microphylla	f
Isolepis nodosus	tu
Isotoma fluviatilis	g
Juncus (various species)	tu
Leptospermum lanigerum	ts
Lythrum salicaria	ss
Marsilea costulifera	g
M. drummondii	g
M. mutica	g
Melaleuca ericifolia	ts-t
M. squarrosa	ts
Mentha australis	g
M. laxiflora	g
Myriophyllum caput-medusae	g
M. variifolium	g
Neopaxia australasica	g
Nymphoides crenata	g
N. geminata	g
Persicaria decipiens	g
Philydrum lanuginosum	tu
Phragmites australis (only for large ponds or dams)	tu
Pratia pedunculata	g
Restio tetraphyllus	tu
Triglochin procera	tu
T. striata	tu
Villarsia exaltata	tu
V. reniformis	tu

Plants for water over 25cm deep

Baumea articulata
Eleocharis sphacelata
Isolepis fluitans
Marsilea (various species)
Myriophyllum papillosum
  M. variifolium
Nelumbo nucifera (best in subtropical or tropical areas)
Nymphoides indica
Ottelia ovalifolia
Potamogeton crispus
  P. ochreatus
  P. perfoliatus
Triglochin procera
Vallisneria spiralis

information on pond and pool construction.

Before considering putting live plants in or beside pools it is worth considering whether you should plant something dead. Yes, dead! My suggestion is that, depending on the pool size, you could place a dead tree trunk or branches in the pool. Birds especially welcome landing perches which are known to be safe from predators such as neighbourhood cats. Don't forget to protect the pool-liner; it can be easily damaged by spiky protuberances. It is a good idea to choose a branch with twigs of differing sizes because different birds have different size claws. If you can find a curved trunk to lie in a pool, partly submerged, you will be amazed how often birds will land on the trunk and then walk down into the water where they proceed to carry out their bathing activities. This is fascinating to observe if you have a protected hide or sheltered place from which you can watch.

A clay-based pool offers many options in terms of which plants you can choose because you don't have to rely on planting in pockets or pots (which are usually needed in concrete or fibreglass pools), but pots of plants may still be used. For information on planting in pots underwater, refer to pages 30–33 in *Water and Wetland Plants for Southern Australia* by Nick Romanowski.

Habitat garden plans

These garden plans provide some suggestions for creating a habitat that appeals to wildlife. You may be able to relate the space you have available to one of these plans or you can tailor them to suit your particular situation. Notice the different planting combinations utilising a wide variety of species — the aim is to provide a year-round food supply, as well as water and shelter. These plants and alternatives are listed in the plant descriptions chapter.

A small inner city house or unit

Key code

Clematis aristata, Billardiera ringens, Passiflora aurantia or *Jasminum suavissimum*

 Anigozanthos species or hybrids

 Scaevola aemula 'Purple Fanfare'

 Bracteantha bracteata

Chrysocephalum apiculatum

Orthrosanthus multiflorus

 Olearia phlogopappa underplanted with *Brachyscome multifida*

 Grevillea lanigera, dwarf

 Correa reflexa, low-spreading form

 Pratia pedunculata in brick paving joints

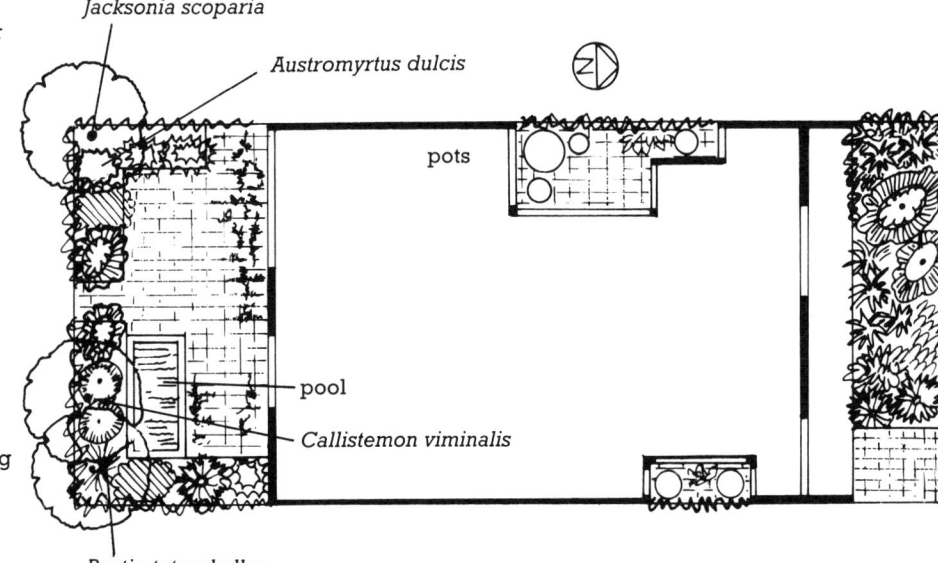

Even a very small garden can be planted with a variety of annuals, climbers and shrubs. This property is only 35m x 6m but it contains all the elements of a wildlife habitat. Plant some *Viola hederacea* in the east and west courtyards and the front yard, and with adequate moisture it will form an outdoor carpet. The pool can be planted with *Nymphoides geminata* and *Myriophyllum variifolium* or *M. papillosum*.

ATTRACTING AND RETAINING WILDLIFE

Large suburban garden backing on to a reserve

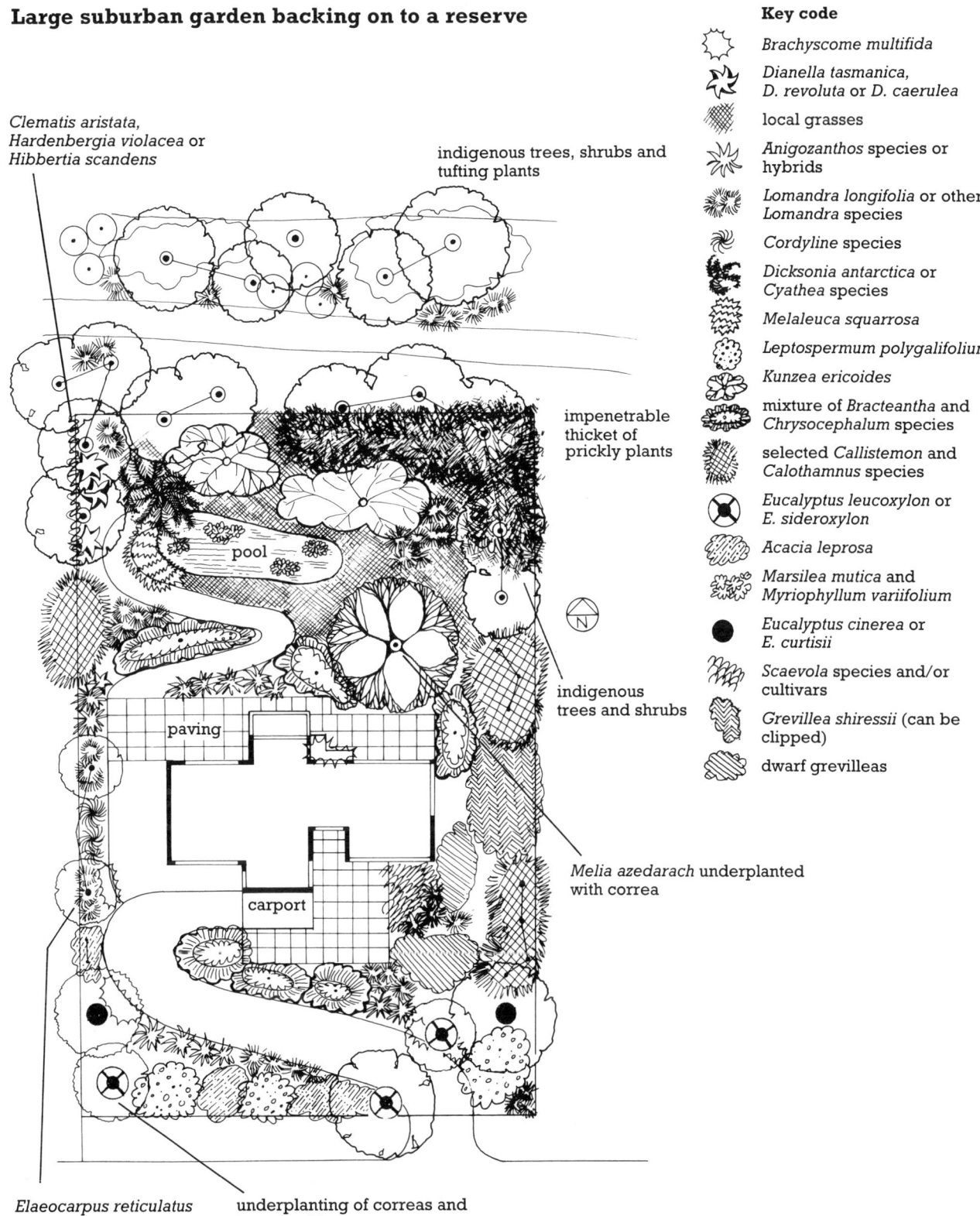

A large garden usually means that you can build a pool (for non-human activity). A pool is a boon for wildlife and will complement your planting scheme. At one end of the pool, you could plant a mixture of *Carex* and *Juncus* species to encourage frogs and aquatic insects to feel right at home.

Key code

 local grass area interplanted with *Chrysocephalum apiculatum* and *Dianella revoluta*

 Passiflora cinnabarina, *Hardenbergia violacea*, *Clematis aristata* or *Billardiera ringens*

 Eucalyptus leucoxylon, *E. sideroxylon*, *E. miniata*, *E. cinerea*, *E. crenulata* or *E. ptychocarpa*

 Hymenosporum flavum

 selected *Callistemon* and/or *Calothamnus* species

 Bracteantha bracteata

 Grevillea juniperina

 ground ferns such as *Doodia* species

 Orthrosanthus species

 Acacia leprosa

Lomandra longifolia or other *Lomandra*

 Anigozanthos species or hybrids

Leptospermum polygalifolium or other tall *Leptospermum* species

 dwarf correas and/or grevilleas

A small suburban garden

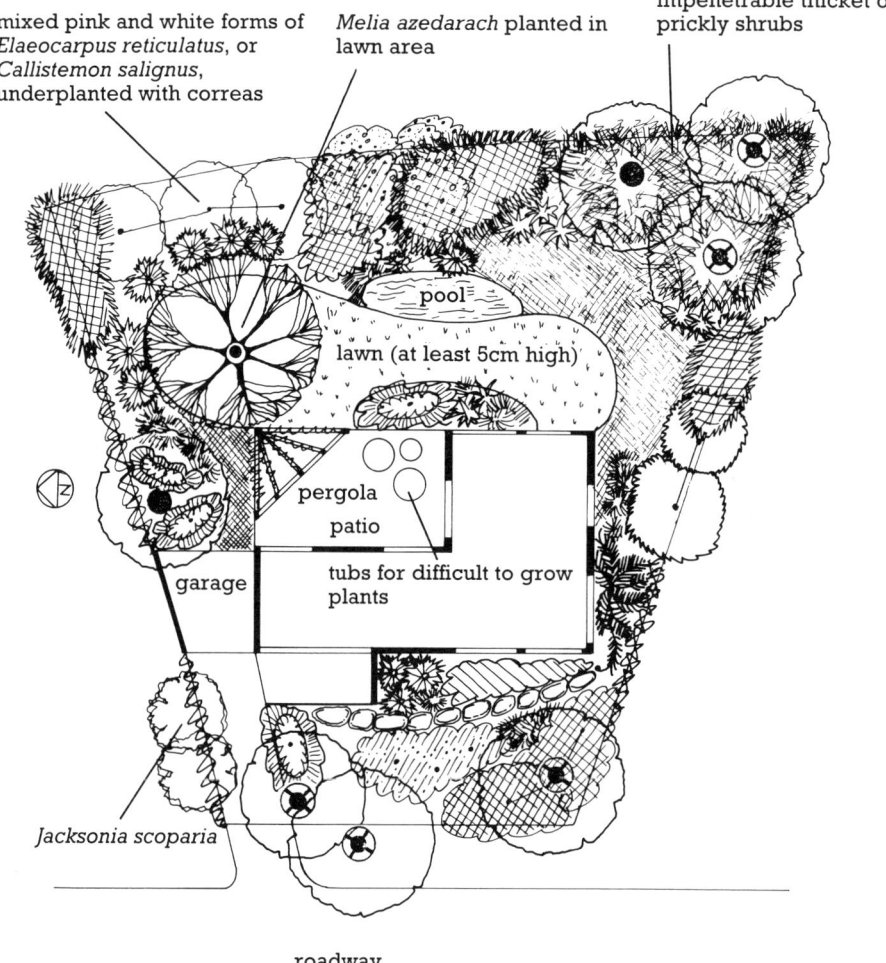

A garden in the suburbs provides ample opportunities to grow a wide range of suitable plants. Note the impenetrable thicket of prickly shrubs in the corner — this area will be a refuge for birds of all kinds. Choose some plants from the list on page 7 for around the pool.

Maintenance — beware of wildlife needs!

Before undertaking any revegetation or reconstruction of an area it is wise to carry out a survey to find out what actually (plants and animals) lives in, or visits the area. You might find that hasty action disrupts resident birds or animals; and it may take many years before they return.

Always keep in mind that every action will have a reaction. If there are many nectar-feeding birds in the garden in winter, always delay pruning of flowering plants such as grevilleas and correas which provide food for them during that time. Try not to remove large areas of vegetation at once. You may wish to remove an invasive jasmine, ivy, morning glory or area of blackberries, but these plants are usually important nesting and resting places for birds and possums. Remove the plants by degrees, and try to replace them as you go with other quick-growing plants that provide similar habitat without being of nuisance value.

Birds in the Australian garden

Native birds

The value of native birds in our gardens can be described purely in terms of their beauty and fascination. Australia is very rich in bird-life, with over 700 indigenous species. Some are absolutely captivating in their visual beauty while others enchant us with the beauty of their songs. For these reasons alone, gardeners deliberately choose to grow bird-attracting species, but there are other added bonuses which are discussed later in this chapter.

Honeyeaters are a fascinating group of native birds. Some species are very small and sometimes very colourful, including: Eastern and Western Spinebills; New Holland Honeyeater; White-eared Honeyeater; White-naped Honeyeater and White-plumed Honeyeater. There are also larger honeyeaters to around 45 cm in length such as the Brush (Little) Wattlebird and Red Wattlebird. All honeyeaters have long, brush-tipped tongues to lick nectar from inside a flower. Tall, slender stems, such as those of *Epacris impressa* (Common Heath), and the flower-stalks of *Anigozanthos* species (Kangaroo Paw), will bend until they almost touch the ground with the weight of some of the larger honeyeaters.

What is this sharp-eyed kookaburra waiting for? (PHOTO: MARION KING)

Bright flashes of vivid colour are provided by the tropical Yellow-bellied Sunbird and by rosellas, lorikeets and galahs, all members of the parrot family. In the morning you may hear the calls of a Grey-shrike Thrush, the carolling of magpies, the apparently ordered raucousness of the kookaburra or the marvellous song of the Grey Butcherbird.

It is not only the birds themselves that are beautiful, we can also admire their nest-building skills. Suspended nests like those of the White-naped Honeyeater and the mud nests of fairy martins are intricately constructed. Conversely, we can only wonder how a tawny frogmouth keeps its eggs in a nest of just a few twigs in a tree fork, let alone hatches and rear the chicks.

You can encourage birds to visit a garden by providing the three major attractions mentioned earlier: food, water and shelter. It is also important that there are suitable nesting sites if you wish the birds to live in your garden, rather than just visit. All of these requirements can be met in suburban or rural gardens.

A natural food supply

You can buy food for distribution to attract native birds but obviously a more satisfactory method and, in the long term, a cheaper one is to provide a natural food source by growing suitable plant species.

Hey Mum! Is that what these chicks are calling out to their Dusky Woodswallow parent? (PHOTO: BILL KING)

Nectar mixture

- Take 4 cups of warm water and mix in 1 cup of raw sugar until dissolved.
- Add a drop of infant vitamin concentrate.
- Pour the mixture into the nectar feeder and store any surplus in the refrigerator.
- Honey should never be used in nectar put out for birds because it can cause diseases if taken by bees back to their hives.

A homemade nectar feeder. Wash the nectar feeder thoroughly between refills. It is recommended that a limited amount of nectar mixture be placed in the feeder every three to four days. Never fill the feeders every day. Remember, it should be only a food supplement for the birds.

Plants with nectar-rich flowers will provide food for honeyeaters and lorikeets. These birds usually frequent tall trees that bear masses of flowers such as *Eucalyptus ficifolia*, *E. calophylla*, *E. eximia* and *Grevillea robusta* but they have also been observed eating the flower-heads of some wattles such as *Acacia schinoides*. Flowering plants also bring insects which in turn are a food source for insect-eating birds including willie wagtails, fantails and thornbills. With careful planning it is possible to grow a range of these species, even in a relatively small area, and achieve flowering throughout the year.

It is not as easy to provide plants which have ripe seed throughout the year. Many seed-eating birds tend to move from area to area as food is available, returning to a garden as different plants are in fruit. To have a few plants which are prolific producers of edible berries is sure to make the difference in encouraging birds such as members of the parrot family.

Supplementary feeding

Supplementary feeding can be provided but it should be exactly that; supplementary, and not given to the extent that birds no longer need or want to seek food for themselves. Feeding can be used to bring birds to a spot in the garden where they can be easily watched. You can supply extra food when there is very little natural food available. Every three to four days is ample!

Never place bird food where the birds are likely to be at risk from predators such as cats, foxes and, to a lesser degree, dogs. A hanging food tray, or elevated table will usually mean the birds will be safe while they eat. A wide smooth-surfaced metal band around posts or legs of supports will prevent cats climbing up them.

If you provide supplementary feeding regularly it is important to arrange for a friend or neighbour to continue the supply when you go away on holidays as it is most likely that birds will be waiting for it.

Nectar feeders

Bottle feeders, to use with a nectar mixture, are fairly widely available and advertised in many of the gardening magazines. They are also relatively simple to construct.

You will need:
- some timber offcuts
- a glass or plastic bottle
- a small plastic bowl with a tightly fitting lid.

Against a timber post or wall construct a ledge shelf to sit the bowl on. Invert the bottle and attach some supports to hold it in place (a nail either side of the bottle with an elastic band, wire or nylon thread stretched from one to the other works well). Cut a circular hole in the lid of the plastic bowl and fit it over the neck of the bottle. Then cut holes in the plastic bowl through which the birds will feed. The position of the holes is determined by placing some water in the bottle, and fixing the upturned bowl on top. Turn the unit upside down and check the level of the water in the bowl. Mark this level on the plastic bowl, then later make about four feeding holes at just above water line. The holes should be only a few millimetres in diameter and can be made fairly easily using a pointed and heated metal object, such as a nail or skewer.

Place the nectar feeder where it is protected from direct sunshine to avoid over-heating the contents. Nectar can be placed in open bowls but this means you have less control over the amount of food available to the birds and an uncovered bowl can also attract unwanted, introduced bees and wasps.

Bird puddings

Bird puddings provide a very effective source of supplementary feeding for native birds. These puddings will be enjoyed by a wide variety of birds, from small wrens and honeyeaters to wattlebirds, butcherbirds and magpies, and can be stored without spoiling for a much longer period than the nectar mixture.

If the pudding is being eaten very quickly, put it in the fridge before you put it out in the garden so that it is firmer and more difficult for the birds to take in large portions. If large birds dominate the bird pudding, try placing it inside a wire crate, large bird-cage or other structure which will allow the smaller birds inside, but keep out larger ones. You can still provide an alternative supply of food for the larger birds but this way you can ensure that smaller species receive a fair share.

Seed puddings

Commercial seed puddings of infinite shapes and sizes are available but many people do not use them because of the glues used in their manufacture. There is a healthy alternative! You can make your own seed puddings bound together with egg-white instead of glue, although these puddings do need cooking to make them stable and, to some degree, waterproof. The mixture consists of six egg-whites which are whisked until fluffy but still of a liquid consistency plus one kilogram of your favourite bird seed (I hope the birds approve!) mixed thoroughly with the egg whites.

You will need some convection ovenproof moulds — the choice of size is up to you. Smaller moulds hold less seed mixture and therefore cook more quickly. Some people find that terracotta pots or saucers are best. Also required is some ovenproof liner to prevent the seed mixture leaking from any holes in the moulds as well as making it easy to release the mix from the moulds. The mix is cooked at 'meringue' temperatures (about 75° Celsius) so microwave plastic wrap is suitable. A piece of wire can be incorporated in the mixture to provide a hanging point — coathanger wire is ideal.

Seed trays and tables

Finches, pigeons, parrots and sparrows are among the birds you can expect to relish a tray spread with suitable seed. Upright tables should have a curved rim, or the seed placed in a seed bowl which curves upwards around the sides, to help prevent the entire contents being quickly scattered onto the ground below.

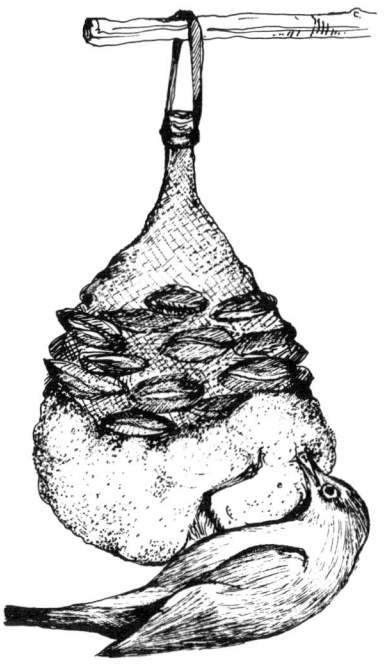

While still warm, the brose meal pudding mixture can be pressed into the openings of banksia cones or pine cones which have shed their seeds — and the cones can then be hung in the garden to provide effective feeders.

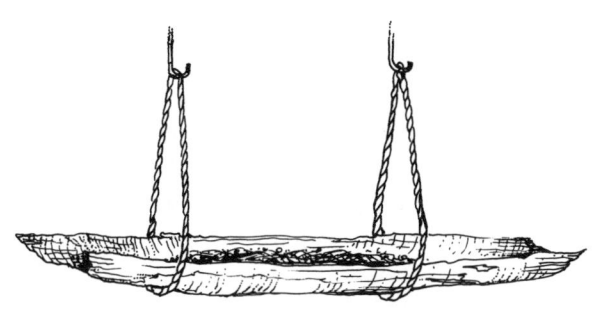

Sections of thick, curved bark or longitudinally split hollow logs can make attractive feeders; they can hang from verandahs or from the branch of a tree.

Dripping, honey and brose meal pudding

- Measure out equal quantities by volume of dripping, honey, brose meal (dried pea flour — obtainable at health food shops), and instant oats (bran or wheat germ can be substituted for oats).
- Warm the dripping and honey, combine well, then add in the brose meal and oats (or substitute).

This mixture can be placed into small pots which are then wired onto trees and shrubs or secured on a bird table.

Plants with pointed, prickly, sharp-edged foliage or thorny stems

Acacia colletioides, 2-3m × 3m
   A. paradoxa, 2-4m × 2-5m
   A. tetragonophylla, 3-5m × 4-6m
   A. triptera, 1-3m × 1-5m
   A. ulicifolia var brownei
      0.5-1m × 1-2m
   A. verticillata, 2-5m × 2-4m
Actinostrobus arenarius, 3-5m × 2-4m
Allocasuarina pinaster, 2-5m × 1-3m
Banksia caleyi, 2-4m × 2-5m
Bursaria spinosa, 3-10m × 1-5m
   (a number of variants)
Callistemon brachyandrus, 1-5m × 1-3m
Citriobatus pauciflorus, 1.5m-2.5m ×
   1-2.5m
Capparis arborea, 2-5m × 1-3m
Coprosma quadrifida, 2-4m × 1-2m
Dryandra polycephala 1-3m × 1-2m
   D. sessilis, 2-6m × 1.5-3.5m
Epacris breviflora, 1-2.5m × 0.5-2m
Gahnia sieberiana, 2-3m × 1-2m
Grevillea aquifolium (shrubby variants),
   1-4m × 2-4m
   G. 'Canberra Gem', 2-4m × 2-5m
   G. 'Clearview David', 2-3m × 2-4m
   G. juniperina, (shrubby variants)
      1-4m × 1.5-4m
   G. paniculata, 1-3m × 2-5m
   G. rivularis, 1-3m × 1-7m
   G. rosmarinifolia (shrubby variants),
      1.5-3m × 2-5m
   G. tripartita, 2-3m × 2-3m
   G. vestita, 2-3m × 2-3.5m
Hakea gibbosa, 2-4m × 1-3m
   H. lissocarpha, 0.6-2m × 1.5-3m
   H. lissosperma, 2-5m × 1-4m
   H. nitida, 1-4m × 1.5-5m
   H. propinqua, 1-3.5m × 1-3m
   H. purpurea, 1-2m × 1-1.5m
   H. sericea, 2-4m × 1-3m
   H. verrucosa, 1.5-2.5m × 2-3m
Labichea lanceolata, 2-3m × 2-3m
Lambertia formosa, 2-3m × 2-3m
Melaleuca styphelioides, 8-20m × 5-10m
   M. pungens, 1-1.5m × 0.6-2m
Microcitrus australasica var. australasica,
   4-8m × 2-5m
Prostanthera spinosa, 0.5-1m × 0.6-1.5m

Seed feeders should also be located where any seed which does fall will not lead to a future weed problem in the garden. So avoid locating seed feeders above or very close to garden beds. And, as with bird puddings, larger birds can sometimes dominate seed tables so it may be necessary for you to use wire mesh or a cage to ensure that smaller birds don't miss out.

There is some concern that regular feeding of introduced birds such as spotted turtle doves, feral pigeons, blackbirds, sparrows etc. gives them the opportunity to increase their populations to the detriment of native birds.

Other food

Once a population of birds is established within a garden you may wish to put out certain little 'extras' from time to time. Scraps of lean meat, dry low-salt cheese, or perhaps marrow bones, sawn in half lengthways and hung in suitable positions. All these foods should be given in small quantities only, and any unused portions removed before they start to deteriorate. Cheese is excellent for providing important calcium; meat is deficient in this element.

When preparing soil for a vegetable garden or other garden beds you are sure to turn up some grubs and other creatures. Birds such as kookaburras and magpies will keep the area under close scrutiny while you are working and quickly swoop at the first opportune moment onto anything that is worth devouring. During and after mowing long grass are also times when many birds will be able to gather displaced insects and small animals. An open compost area is also a valuable food source area for birds.

Water

A year-round source of water is of prime importance in any garden designed to attract native birds. Birds need water for drinking and bathing. The water should be as clean as possible and cool.

A shallow pool can be incorporated as an attractive feature in the garden and at the same time provide water for the birds. If the pool is small, cats can be a problem at ground level but in a larger pond a rock or log, away from the outer edge, will provide a moderately safe perching site for the birds as they drink. A selection of waterplants (see pages 7–8) near the edge will provide refuge for aquatic life such as frogs, which in turn will control water-breeding insects such as mosquitoes.

A broad dish in a raised position above ground level for protection from predators can also be a good source of water, providing the water is topped up as necessary. Do not locate containers such as this in direct sunshine; shallow water can become quite hot during warm, sunny days. Ready-made bird baths are available from nurseries and garden supply centres or you can make a masterpiece of your own!

Shelter for refuge and nesting sites

Like all creatures, birds will be prepared to stay within an environment if they feel comfortable and safe. This applies particularly to many of the smaller native species.

Plants with spines or sharply pointed leaves provide a place of refuge, allowing small birds to shelter where larger birds or other predators such as cats will be unable to follow. Plants which are bushy right to ground level will ensure that there is protection for some of the birds which stay within the lower storey of vegetation. Prickly plants are often also used for nesting by many of the small birds.

Nesting sites

Nesting materials are an important consideration and plants such as the paperbarked melaleucas, including *Melaleuca linariifolia* and *M. quinquenervia*, are popular as source material for nest construction. The papery bark of *Leptospermum laevigatum* is also widely used, as is material from stringybarked eucalypts and the string-like bark from *Acacia inophloia* and *Allocasuarina inophloia*. Dried grass and the foliage of rushes and similar plants is also very useful nesting material.

We have watched more than one hemp doormat outside our home being demolished by nest-making birds and we never remove spiders' webs under the eaves for the same reason. If you have birds nesting in the garden, it may be worthwhile keeping any scraps of old hessian, raw sheep wool, or similar fibrous material, and leaving them where the birds can gather pieces as required during the nesting period.

Birds such as kingfishers, kookaburras, owls, treecreepers, budgerigars, galahs, rosellas and other members of the parrot family like to build their nests in tree hollows. Tree hollows form mainly in very mature eucalypts, such as *Eucalyptus camaldulensis* and *E. ovata*. It is important that some older trees are retained in all areas of natural bushland even if they are no longer vigorous, or possibly even if they're dead, as these provide many valuable nesting sites for animals as well as for birds.

Materials and equipment list

1 × 60–100 litre plastic drum (or an old gravity-feed hot water tank)
1 × **ball valve** (as in toilet cistern)
1 × **gate valve** (to suit pipe size) plus plumbing fittings
1 × **suitable length of high or low pressure plastic pipe or hose to connect tank to water supply**
1 × **short length of copper pipe for the spout** (optional)
1 × **bird bath** (commercial or homemade)

A garden that is unsuitable for a permanent pool can overcome this deficiency by having a permanently dripping source of water. This virtually guarantees a constant stream of bird visitors. You will need to install some equipment but this should not be an expensive undertaking as secondhand and homemade materials can be used. Try to camouflage the tank with foliage.

In a suburban garden it is not easy, within a short space of years, to provide tree hollows, even with the selection of appropriate species. You might be able to buy hollow logs to tie onto other trees or special nesting boxes can be constructed. Nesting boxes or logs should be placed in a protected position away from very hot sunshine and the entrance should face away from hot or cold winds. The nesting boxes should be around 5–6m above ground level and should be located with adequate protection from cats, rats and other predators. A wide band of metal around a pole or tree trunk below the nest will ensure that these creatures cannot climb up to the nest. It is worth keeping in mind that such treatment of posts can look unsightly if not done well.

Constructed nesting boxes should provide protection from rain but still allow good ventilation. The opening should be just large enough for entry by the birds for which it is designed. Some drainage holes should be drilled in the base in case rainwater seeps in. A layer of around 2–6cm of sawdust, dried semi-decayed leaves or a dried termite bed may be placed in the base of nest boxes.

Nesting boxes are available commercially, or you may like to construct your own, using the illustrations in the side columns as a guide. Members of the parrot family and treecreepers usually prefer vertical nesting sites while kookaburras and other kingfishers like a horizontal log or nest box. Members of the owl family differ in their preferences too.

Mounds of earth, compost and sawdust or sloping embankments that have crevices in the soil or crevices beneath rocks are often sought as nesting sites by pardalotes. They enlarge the crevices or dig tunnels and make a lovely softly-lined nest at the end of the tunnel. Because they can nest at close to ground level it may be necessary to provide protection from predators. This can be done by enveloping the mound or part thereof with chicken wire, securely fastened to prohibit penetration by undesirable animals.

The Bird Observers Club of Australia, 183 Springvale Rd, Nunawading, Vic. 3131, can supply Australia-wide a pamphlet entitled 'Nest Boxes for Australian Birds', in which the following dimensions are given as a guideline as well as other information.

Bird	Suggested box size	Suggested entrance hole diameter
rosellas	40cm+ deep x 12–15cm wide	7-12cm
Striated Pardalote	20cm+ x 12–15cm (H or V)	2.5–3.5cm
Laughing Kookaburra	40cm+ long x 15–30cm deep and wide (H)	8-12cm
Red-rumped parrot	40cm long x 10-15cm wide (preferably H)	7-12cm+
Treecreepers	10-15cm deep x 9-15cm wide (preferably V)	5-8cm
Grey Shrike-thrush	15-20cm square x 20–30cm deep (open-fronted box preferred, not in direct light)	15cm
Owlet Nightjar	15cm square but can be deeper (preferably V)	7-12cm
Grey Teal*, Chestnut Teal*	45cm x 30cm	8-10cm
Black Duck*	45cm x 30cm	12cm
Pink-eared Duck	a platform	

* nesting box is ideally situated on an island or affixed to a pole in a pool, dam or lake.

Orientation of box: H=horitzonal ⬜; V= vertical ▯

Many of us would yearn to have this quaint and appealing Feather-tailed Glider visiting or inhabiting our properties. Such a visitor is a faint possibility if forest or woodland is nearby, and especially if your garden has some tall trees. (PHOTO: BILL KING)

Crescent Honeyeater gathering nectar from *Banksia spinulosa*. This banksia can grow to about 6 m, although dwarf forms of 0.5-1 m are available, and it can be in flower from February to July. (PHOTO: BILL KING)

A homemade nesting box in a eucalypt will suit clucky rosellas in spring. You may need to climb up and give the box a clean-out in autumn, so make sure you locate nesting boxes in an easy-to-reach spot.

Grevillea 'Ned Kelly' is tremendously long-flowering and very attractive to all nectar-feeding creatures. This small shrub grows in sub-tropical to temperate regions and prefers sunny, well-drained spots. Regular pruning of old woody stems helps promote new bushy growth.

Pest control

Enjoying native birds in your garden means that you will need to accept the presence of some insects and other creatures you may previously have regarded as garden pests! As the old saying goes — you can't have your cake and eat it too. You will inevitably find a few chewed leaves on favourite plants but, for the continued safety of the birds, you should avoid using pesticides. The bonus is that pesticides are rarely needed in a garden if there is a population of permanent or visiting native birds. Birds are really very efficient aids to natural pest control. And, by not using pesticides we avoid passing them on through the food chain. Pesticides transferred through the food chain can severely deplete bird and animal populations. We may also avoid detrimental effects on the environment and our own personal health.

Insects form part of the diet of all native birds. Fantails, flycatchers, robins, silver-eyes, wrens and a number of other quite common birds are primarily insect-eaters, and feed on a wide variety of garden creatures, including pests such as aphids and scale. Honeyeaters do not live on nectar alone, but also eat many small creatures. Insects provide a source of protein in the honeyeater's diet. The smaller honeyeaters such as New Holland Honeyeater and White-plumed Honeyeater eagerly devour many of the tiny insects within the garden, while larger honeyeaters such as the Wattlebirds prefer to feed on larger creatures such as beetles, moths and cicadas. If passion-vine hoppers are proliferating you're sure to hear the constant clacking of wattlebird beaks.

Studies of red wattlebirds in Melbourne showed that they can suffer from thiamine (vitamin B_1) deficiency. This occurs indirectly because the birds no longer migrate to warmer climates during southern winters. With many plants producing nectar-bearing flowers in winter and the continuing supplementary feeding by humans the birds are content to stay. However, their insect intake is reduced because there is less insect activity during cold weather. It is therefore imperative to have plants in gardens which attract insects as well as mulched areas to provide an ideal habitat for insects and small animals.

Rosellas and other parrots will often systematically process plants with gall infestations in the leaves and small branchlets. Galls are caused by the egg-laying activities of various wasps and other insects. The birds break apart the galls to eat the insect-larvae inside and create valuable mulch with the remnants of their meal. These and other birds such as butcherbirds, kookaburras and magpies will also eagerly seek out any grubs, caterpillars and snails crawling on trees and shrubs or at ground level. Sawfly larvae, also known as Spit-grubs can congregate in large clusters during the day on branches and trunks of eucalypts only to go forth at night and devour large amounts of foliage. There are few birds who find them to their taste but, fortunately, they are part of the diet of gang gang cockatoos and black-faced cuckoo-shrikes.

Plant pollination

The relationship between native birds and plants is one which benefits both, rather than being simply one-sided. Plant pollination, or the transferring of pollen from one flower or plant to another, leads to the formation of seeds and fruits which in turn provide food for wildlife.

It is commonly thought that many Australian plants are pollinated by the introduced European honey-bees. In some cases this is true, but Australian plants did not evolve in an environment which included these creatures and so many plants have adapted to quite different methods of pollination.

Plants for nectar-feeding birds (honeyeaters)

Plant names asterisked are discussed in detail in the text.

Code for plant groups

tu = tussock or clump-forming plants
g = groundcovers and low shrubs to 1m tall
ss = shrubs, around 1-3m tall
ts = tall shrubs, 3-6m tall
t = trees, 6m plus
c = climber

Angophora species*	t
Anigozanthos species*	tu
Banksia species*	ts
Beaufortia species*	ss
*Billardiera longiflora**	c
Callistemon species*	ss-t
*Calothamnus quadrifidus**	ss-ts
*Castanospermum australe**	t
Correa species	g-t
*C. lawrenciana**	ts-t
*C. 'Mannii'**	ss-ts
*C. reflexa**	g-ss
Doryanthes species*	tu
*Epacris impressa**	ss
*E. longiflora**	ss
Eucalyptus species	t
*E. curtisii**	t
*E. ficifolia**	t
*E. leucoxylon**	t
E. megacornuta	t
*E. ptychocarpa**	t
*E. sideroxylon**	t
Grevillea species*	g-t
G. arenaria	ss
G. banksii and hybrids*	ss-ts
*G. juniperina**	g-ss
G. 'Poorinda Constance'	ss
G. 'Robyn Gordon'	ss
Hakea species	ss-ts
*H. laurina**	ts
*Hymenosporum flavum**	t
Melaleuca species*	ss-t
*M. elliptica**	ts
M. leucadendra	t
Regelia velutina	ts
*Schefflera actinophylla**	ts-t
*Stenocarpus sinuatus**	t
*Telopea speciosissima**	ts-t
*Templetonia retusa**	ts
*Xanthostemon chrysanthus**	ts-t

Red wattlebirds require about five hundred small insects per day to maintain good health

Plants for insect-eating birds

Plant names asterisked are discussed in detail in the text.

Code for plant groups

tu = tussock or clump-forming plants
g = groundcovers and low shrubs to 1m tall
ss = shrubs, around 1-3m tall
ts = tall shrubs, 3-6m tall
t = trees, 6m plus
c = climber

Acacia species	ss-t
A. howittii	ts-t
*A. verniciflua**	ss-t
*Bracteantha bracteata**	ss
*Buckinghamia celsissima**	ts-t
*Bursaria spinosa**	ts-t
*Callicoma serratifolia**	ts-t
*Ceratopetalum gummiferum**	ts-t
*Chrysocephalum apiculatum**	g-ss
Eucalyptus species*	ss-t
*Eupomatia laurina**	ts-t
*Grevillea acanthifolia**	ss
*G. crithmifolia**	ss
*Jacksonia scoparia**	ss-ts
Leptospermum species*	ss-ts
*Leucophyta brownii**	g-ss
Melaleuca species	ss-t
*M. decussata**	ss-ts
M. viminea ssp. *viminea**	ss-ts
*Melia azedarach**	t
Olearia species*	ss
*Orthrosanthus multiflorus**	tu
Phebalium species	ss
Thryptomene calycina	ss
*T. saxicola**	ss
*Viminaria juncea**	ss-ts

The showy petals of larger flowering plants entice pollinators to visit and the petals also act as landing platforms. In these cases the pollinators are usually insects, such as hover-flies and bees, of which there are many Australian species. Other flowers encourage their pollinators through their floral fragrances. There are quite a large number of white or cream flowers which emit their fragrances as twilight begins or in the evening, and are pollinated by night-flying moths.

One of the more unusual plant adaptations occurs within the orchid family, where the flower of some species mimics the sexual odours of a female wasp. The male is encouraged to the flower and, in an attempt to mate with it, pollination of the flower occurs. This process is known as pseudocopulation. Species which have evolved in this manner include *Cryptostylis subulatus*, which is visited by Ichneumon wasps while species of *Arthrochilus*, some *Caladenia* species, *Chiloglottis*, *Drakaea* and *Spiculaea* are visited by Brachinid wasps.

The flower petals of a large number of Australian plants are either minute or absent, as in eucalypts and bottlebrushes, where showy stamens act as lures for insects and birds. Yet other plants have petals which are fused to form long, narrow tubes or bells, for instance: correas; grevilleas; heaths and kangaroo paws. Many of these plants are pollinated primarily by nectar-feeding birds, with brush-tipped tongues which uncurl from their long, narrow beaks.

In the process of visiting the flowers to drink the nectar, pollen is deposited, usually on the head or throat of the bird, and then transferred to the stigma of the next flower on its progressive dinner route. It is not uncommon to see birds feeding from native plants with their heads quite golden in appearance from the dustings of pollen. In the natural environment cross-pollination is a vital feature in the survival of plant species and the pollinators play a very important role in the process of seed production and subsequent plant generations.

In gardens which contain a range of plants that have originated from assorted locations and habitats, it is most likely that hybridisation has occurred. So it is quite possible that seed dispersed or taken from garden plants and allowed to germinate may result in plants that are not the same as the plant from which it was collected. This is how plants like *Grevillea* 'Robyn Gordon' originated.

Plants for seed-eating birds

Acacia species*	ss-t
*Alectryon subcinereus**	ts
*Austromyrtus dulcis**	ss
*Callicarpa pedunculata**	s
*Coprosma quadrifida**	ss-ts
*Elaeocarpus reticulatus**	t
Eucalyptus species*	ss-t
*Eugenia reinwardtiana**	ss-ts
Ficus species*	t
(Ficus are notable for their enlarged fruit-like receptacles)	
*Kunzea ericoides**	ts-t
Polyscias species*	ts-t
*Solanum aviculare**	ss-ts
Syzygium species*	t

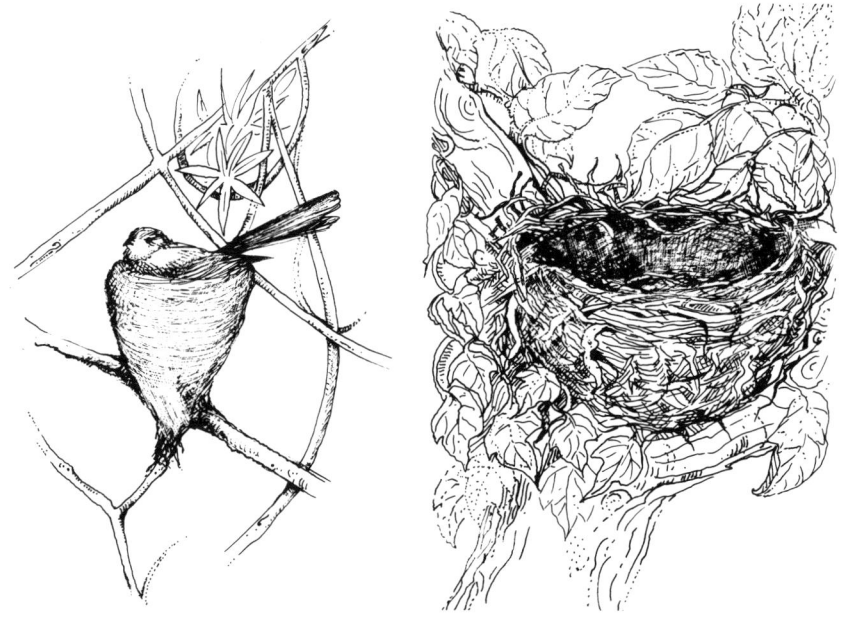

A fantail's wine glass-shaped nest and a blackbird's nest.

Bird problems

The majority of native birds cause very little, if any, annoyance to gardeners or others within the house or neighbourhood.

Members of the parrot family can cause a few harsh words when they are seen feasting on fruit or fruit-tree buds and, were it not for their beauty, this annoyance would no doubt be even greater. In domestic situations bird-netting is available for throwing over trees during the fruiting season. It's possible for birds to become tangled so nets must be monitored regularly. Problems are less likely to occur if the netting is white and readily visible to the birds and is pulled taut over a frame or a series of stakes and is anchored or staked at the base. Birds will often be kept away if pieces of aluminium foil or other shiny objects are tied to tree branches.

Some of the parrot family such as the Yellow-tailed Black Cockatoo may damage plants which have borers; parrots have a wonderful knack of locating borers, often knocking their beaks against the trunks or branches and if a hollow-sounding resonance results, their fantastically strong beaks quickly tear away the outer wood to reveal a tasty morsel. This action can result in permanent damage to plants especially if they are very young.

The introduced blackbird presents one of the major bird problems in the garden, scratching out and destroying seedlings or young plants, scattering mulch and, in particular, spreading the seeds of many noxious or feral weeds such as blackberry, boneseed, Shining Coprosma, holly, Sweet Pittosporum and ivy. Blackbirds, together with indian mynahs, sparrows and starlings are often aggressive towards other birds, including native birds in their own habitat, and can force some of the native birds out of the area. If you can find nests containing eggs of these introduced birds they can be removed to prevent further spread. If you find supplementary food (see page 12) is being dominated by introduced species, you'll have to stop the feeding.

Blackbirds usually build their nests in densely-foliaged shrubs or trees and on occasions on protected overhangs of buildings. Indian mynahs and starlings generally build nests on or in buildings and they are very efficient in finding the smallest of holes or crevices. Even guttering downpipes are used by these birds. Sparrows also prefer the environs of buildings.

Birds find it easier to recognise windows if self-adhesive bird-shapes or decorative, colourful transfers are attached.

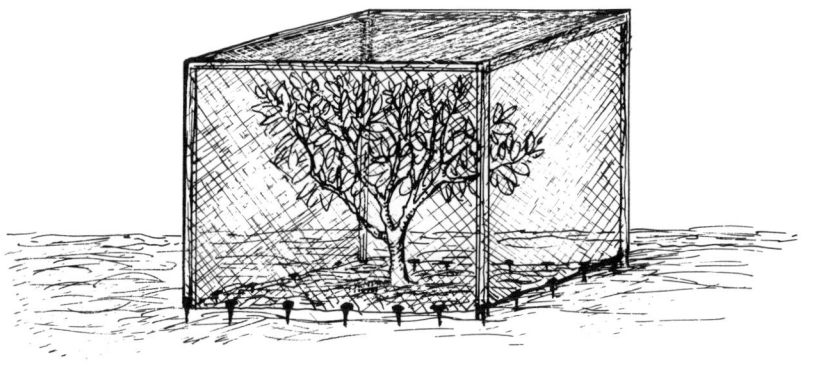

Fruit trees such as pears can be protected from hungry birds with netting. Putting up nets is a bit of a chore, so you may be prepared to live with some damaged fruit. Collapsable frames are available.

Birds and windows

A large expanse of window can be a hazard for fast-flying birds, especially if the windows provide a view through the house from one side to the other. That is how, sometimes, birds assume there is a clear flight-path but neglect to recognise the transparent intervening glass. Impact with the glass in full flight can result in injury or death. This problem can be alleviated by making the window distinctive, either by having blinds or curtains drawn closed on one side of the house or by placing objects on the window.

Butterflies, moths, other insects and spiders

This is an Emperor Gum Moth; notice the distinguishing feather or fern-like antennae. (PHOTO: BILL KING)

Butterflies or moths?

Butterflies and moths are very closely related but, fortunately, it is quite easy to tell them apart. Look at their wing position: butterflies usually rest with their wings folded together in an upright position, whereas the wings of moths are usually folded along the body over the abdomen in tent-like fashion. The antennae are different too: butterflies have club-like antennae while a moth's antennae are somewhat feather-like. Butterflies usually fly and feed during the day and so, perhaps, are more commonly observed in gardens than moths, which are active after the sun has gone down. Moths are most noticeable in the evenings and are frequently the pollinators of plants which are open at night and have a sweet fragrance.

There are around 20 000 species of butterflies throughout the world, with 400 or more found in Australia. About half the Australian species do not occur elsewhere. Moths do tend to be the poor relations of butterflies because they are thought to lack the more dramatic characteristics of butterflies. I think this is misleading — many moths have superlative features. And do you know that there are about 20 000 species of moths in Australia alone!

Migratory habits

One of the most famous Australian moths, the Bogong Moth, was an important source of food for Koori people. This moth is now well known for its fantastic migratory exodus in summer from breeding grounds near the south-eastern coast to the Australian Alps, returning later in the year to the coast.

The Monarch or Wanderer is a fascinating migratory butterfly. In Australia it is found right down the east coast from northern Australia, and around to Adelaide and the southern Flinders Ranges in South Australia. There have also been sightings in Tasmania, Western Australia and Northern Territory. This tan, black and white species originally came from North America, where it has a regular migratory pattern, moving southwards during autumn to spend winter in California, Florida, Texas and Mexico. Over winter they gather together in dense colonies on specific trees, numbering in the thousands, and have become a major tourist attraction. The Wanderer can fly long distances, over land or water, and has now become established in Central and South America, parts of Europe, Australia, Malaysia, New Guinea, New Zealand and most of the Pacific Islands. Although specimens have been observed flying hundreds of miles out to sea, it is thought that distribution across some of the vast distances is likely to have been aided by international shipping.

The Monarch or Wanderer Butterfly can cover enormous distances in its short lifespan.

Beauty and variety

The beauty of butterflies is a combination of both colour and movement. Butterflies are more abundant in tropical regions, where they reach a peak in terms of size and spectacular colours. In temperate regions the colour tones are often subtle but still extremely attractive. Even species which lack bright colours are still fascinating to watch as they flit from flower to flower, pausing to drink nectar. Their bodies are small and their wings sturdy, even though they may appear so fragile.

It is not only the adult butterfly that can be attractive; the chrysalis (or cocoon) from which the adult emerges can be intricately shaped or colourful, like a jewel adorning plants in the garden. The chrysalis of the Australian Admiral is greyish-brown and can have silver or gold markings; the Macleay's Swallowtail chrysalis is bright green with yellow, narrow elongated markings.

As with bird-attracting plants, it is often not until we actually have a butterfly-attracting species in the garden, whether by design or accident, that we come to appreciate the added dimension of beauty these creatures can provide. Try sitting quietly, perhaps with a good book and a camera, near an everlasting daisy on a sunny day. You may find you do very little reading but you may take some marvellous photos. Butterflies tend to be less concerned with human presence than many of the native birds and can therefore be observed close at hand, if you are sitting or standing still. If you are trying to chase and capture a butterfly it can be a very different story!

An Australian Admiral Butterfly alights on *Pimelea ciliata*.

Life cycles and ecology

The life cycle or metamorphosis of a butterfly or moth has four distinct stages: the egg; the caterpillar; the chrysalis or cocoon; and the adult butterfly or moth. The life cycle of some species may be completed within a period of weeks while for others it may take a number of years. If the prevailing conditions are not suitable, a halt or dormancy period in the life cycle may occur: when the conditions are favourable the cycle restarts.

After the mating of male and female adults, eggs are laid by the female. The eggs vary considerably in shape, from species to species, and can be disc-like, spherical, tapered or elongated. A very large number of eggs are usually produced, but only few survive to maturity as butterflies or fully fledged moths. Some eggs are parasitised by small wasps, or become part of the food chain when they are eaten by a variety of other insects and birds. The eggs are nearly always laid on the food plant of the particular butterfly species, and as the caterpillar or larva hatches it has an immediate source of nourishment, literally at its feet.

The caterpillar or larva has a healthy appetite and feeds by chewing on foliage of the host plant or plants. It increases in size several times during this stage and must shed its smaller skin several times. Some butterfly or moth caterpillars stay hidden during the day, feeding mainly at night. Other moth caterpillars, which are brightly coloured or look fearsome enough to scare predators, such as the Emperor Gum Moth, feed openly during daylight.

Gardeners are often concerned when they find caterpillars on favourite plants. It is true that caterpillars will chew leaves and new growth but it should also be borne in mind that many butterfly and moth species are very selective about food plants: if we grow plants to attract these creatures it is only logical and we must accept that some leaves are likely to be chewed. Generally the eating of new growth by caterpillars does serve a useful purpose as a form of natural pruning, and often results in bushier, more compact plants.

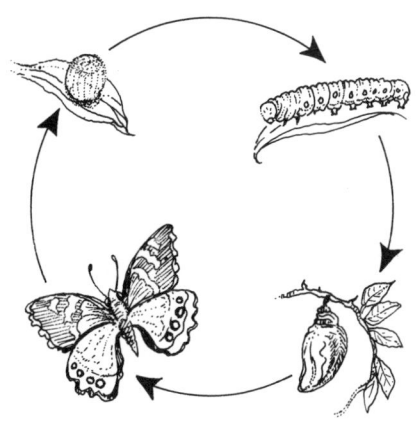

The life cycle of a butterfly or moth: egg; caterpillar; chrysalis; and adult.

Plants for butterflies and moths

Plants asterisked are discussed in detail in the text.

Code for plant groups

tu = tussock or clump-forming plants
g = groundcovers and low shrubs to 1m tall
ss = shrubs, around 1-3m tall
ts = tall shrubs, 3-6m tall
t = trees, 6m plus
c = climber

Acacia species* (most)	g-t
Actinotus helianthi *	ss
Alphitonia excelsa *	t
Amyema (Mistletoes, aerial parasites)	
Angophora species* (most)	t
Aristilochia species (most)	c
Banksia species* (many)	ss-t
Brachychiton species*	t
Brachyscome multifida *	g
Bracteantha bracteata *	g-ss
Breynia species* (most)	ss-ts
Buckinghamia celsissima *	ts-t
Bursaria spinosa *	ts-t
Callicoma serratifolia *	ts-t
Callistemon species* (most)	ss-t
Calytrix tetragona *	ss
Carex fascicularis *	tu
Cassia species* (most)	g-ss
Chrysocephalum species*	g
Craspedia glauca *	tu
Doryanthes species*	tu
Eucalyptus species* (most)	ts-t
Euodia elleryana *	t
Exocarpus cupressiformis *	t
Grevillea species* (most)	g-t
Hakea species* (most)	ss-t
Hoya species	g/c
Hymenanthera dentata *	ts
Hypocalymma species*	ss
Jacksonia scoparia *	ss-ts
Jasminum lineare	c
J. suavissimum *	g/c
Kunzea species* (most)	g-ts
Leptospermum species* (most)	g-t
Lomandra species* (most)	tu
Lomatia species* (most)	ss-t
Melaleuca species* (most)	ss-t
Microcitrus species*	ss-ts
Microlaena stipoides	tu
Morinda species*	g/c/ss
Olearia species* (most)	ss-ts
Passiflora species*	c
Poa species* (most)	tu
Pomaderris species* (most)	ss-t
Pultenaea juniperina *	ss-ts
Senna species* (most)	ss-ts
Tasmannia species*	ss-ts
Thelionema caespitosa *	tu
Wahlenbergia species*	tu/g
Wilkiea species*	ss-t

Unfortunately, some moth caterpillars also have a well-known liking for clothing and carpets.

In a native garden the web of life may be in a very healthy state. If you have a population of native birds, a percentage of the caterpillars will never reach the stage of being adult butterflies. The use of insecticidal sprays is usually not necessary and, in fact, should be avoided in all but extreme situations as it can have a catastrophic and lasting effect on the food chain.

At the completion of its larval stage, the butterfly caterpillar undertakes a complete change (metamorphosis). During this time the caterpillar envelops itself and changes to a smooth pupa or chrysalis. A pupal case is usually spun and this hardens around the pupating larva. In several species the case is camouflaged or it may be brightly coloured to deter predators. The moth caterpillar often becomes enveloped by a silken cocoon. After a period of time adult insects emerge from the chrysalis. Some species undertake this transformation attached to host plants, while others seek a sheltered position in leaf litter.

When the metamorphosis is complete, the pupal case splits and the adult butterfly slowly emerges. Its wings are soft and folded and it is not until blood is pumped between the membranes that the wings gradually expand and harden. The adult butterfly, possibly the only one out of a hundred or more eggs laid, is then ready for its first flight. The adults no longer chew on the foliage of host plants; butterflies and moths drink the nectar supplied by flowers of a variety of different plants. The male often gets sidetracked and flies in search of the female and the cycle of reproduction begins once more!

Encouraging butterflies and moths to the garden

The range of butterfly and moth species you can hope to attract to your garden depends primarily on where you live because their distribution is affected by climatic features, including temperature and rainfall. Their distribution is also controlled by the availability of host plants which provide food and shelter for the caterpillars and other plants which produce nectar for the adult insects. Caterpillars may live in association with only one, or a small number, of plant species while others have adapted to a much wider range.

If you are in the process of developing a new garden or refurbishing an old garden and wish to attract butterflies and moths it is worth observing their activity in nearby gardens or bushland. You can make a note of the food plants used or being visited and perhaps even identify the species of butterfly and moth in the area. Information about the butterfly and moth species native to a region can be obtained from specialised publications (see Further Reading, page 63). Other sources of information include entomological societies and field naturalists clubs in the various states of Australia.

It is more likely that butterflies and moths will visit and perhaps stay to breed if you have a garden which has some wild or informal areas. A heavily manicured garden does not usually appeal for breeding purposes to butterflies and moths. And always remember that regular use of pesticides will quickly deplete a garden of any breeding insects.

The presence of grasses and other tussocking or clumping plants such as dianellas, sword-sedges and various rushes is extremely beneficial. The larvae of some skipper butterflies, for example, feed only on the foliage of *Lomandra* species. Some moth larvae feed on the roots of *Danthonia* species (Wallaby Grasses). Loose mulch which contains plenty of curled eucalypt bark and leaf litter is important too as some butterflies, but more often moths, pupate in such materials. Moths often seek crevices to rest or pupate so it is worthwhile growing trees which have rough and deeply furrowed bark as do the ironbarks, *Eucalyptus sideroxylon* and *E. tricarpa*. Wattles are especially valuable for butterfly populations as their flowers are very attractive to these insects.

There is a strongly inculcated notion that mistletoe plants are harmful to their host. This is true but it is balanced by the fact that mistletoes are extremely valuable plants for butterfly conservation. The larvae of species such as the Imperial White Butterfly, *Delias harpalyce* rely heavily on the Weeping Mistletoe, *Amyema pendula* as a food source.

Not all the butterfly and moth food plants are Australian native species as some of these insects have a wide natural distribution with a range of different host plants in different locations. Some butterflies and moths are attracted to introduced. One excellent example is the Monarch or Wanderer butterfly, referred to in the section on migratory habits. It feeds on host plants from three families, including the genus *Asclepias*, with species commonly known as swan plants or milkweeds. As suitable food plants have become established (often as weeds) throughout various areas of the world, the range of the Wanderer butterfly has been extended accordingly.

Many *Buddleia* species are highly regarded for their nectar-bearing flowers and consequently they are commonly called butterfly flowers. *Buddleia davidii*, *B. alternifolia* and *B. salvifolia* are good butterfly-attractants.

Plant pollination

Like the honeyeating birds, butterflies and moths are attracted to tubular flowers, but they look for flowers which are usually significantly smaller, for example *Pimelea* species. Butterflies also frequent daisies, leptospermums, eucalypts, grevilleas, banksias and bottlebrushes as well as many grasses and other plants.

In feeding on the nectar of flowers, adult butterflies and moths serve a very useful role as distributors of pollen. A potent two-way relationship exists between plant and insect. As a butterfly or moth lands on a flower its senses are stimulated through taste buds located on its feet. The insect then unrolls its long coiled tongue or proboscis to drink the nectar. In many species the depth of the floral tube matches the length of the insect's tongue, so that the creature must probe the flower just sufficiently to brush against the pollen-bearing anthers and the stigma. As it visits the next flower cross-pollination is achieved.

Butterflies are able to recognise different colours and many of the plants adapted to pollination by these creatures have pink, yellow or white flowers. Moths are strongly attracted to white or cream flowers, especially those with a fragrance which is most noticeable in the evenings.

Desirable insects and beetles

The insect world includes a fascinating array of creatures, many of which are important allies in the garden. Remember, the more diverse the vegetation in your garden, the more diverse the array of insects you will attract and the greater the likelihood of achieving ecological balance.

The best way to increase your insect population overnight is to create a small permanent water pond or pool. The difference will be noticeable almost immediately. Of course, you may have already established a pool with vegetation in it as well as around the margins in order to attract birds and

Cross-pollination occurs as butterflies move from flower to flower.

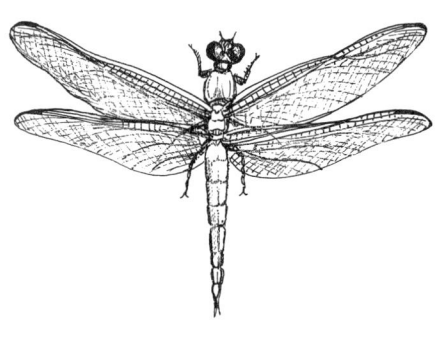
Dragon fly

Hover fly

Praying mantid

other creatures. Most insects will respond positively to a range of water plants and water margin plants.

If your pool dries out in summer you may not be pleased to see the soil beginning to crack. Do not despair, there is some value in those cavities as they will become home to many land-loving insects and small creatures.

Dragonflies and damsel flies

Many insects, such as the beautiful dragonflies and damsel flies, require plenty of submerged and emergent vegetation in a pool. The adults lay their eggs on plants below the waterline and then the nymphs (immature adults without wings) develop and eventually climb up the vegetation, out of the water — this can take a number of years. At all stages in their life cycle dragonflies and damsel flies are carnivorous and extremely valuable in controlling insect explosions including mosquito larvae in pools.

Hover-flies

On a warm, sunny day flowering boronias, tea-trees, waxflowers and many other plants are often the centre of attention for some small insects, aptly named hover-flies. These insects, which are black with bands of yellow-green or deep orange, are smaller than bees and often mistaken as wasps. They can be solitary or there may be quite a number hovering together above a flowering plant. Their fast-moving wings are virtually invisible. Helicopters could take lessons from them in manoeuvrability.

Their hovering activities are not without benefit in the garden, as they are fantastic pollinators of plants. In return, they gather large quantities of nectar from the flowers. Hover-fly larvae are green, plumpish, somewhat slug-like and have an excellent appetite for aphids. These helpful insects can improve the appearance of your plants by reducing the loss of sap to aphids.

Praying mantids

Praying mantids, from the insect family *Mantidae* are also known as praying mantises, after the genus *Mantis*, to which some belong. Praying mantids are commonly seen sitting in a prayer-like position — the front pair of legs raised and ready to seize any insect victim which ventures too close. Each foreleg has a set of sharp tooth-like spikes to help secure the prey very firmly.

This group of insects is readily distinguished by their ability to turn their head: an action which is unique in the insect world! They are relatively large insects, often green in colour, although some species are greyish or brown.

The diet of the praying mantid consists of a large range of insects and other small creatures including various flies, wasps, bees, crickets, grasshoppers and spiders; many of these are regarded as garden pests. They do not eat foliage — it is the grasshoppers and stick insects, with which the praying mantids are sometimes confused, that are avid devourers of foliage. In turn, praying mantids provide a food source for birds, lizards and small mammals, while their eggs are eaten by crickets and often parasitised by wasps.

In most Australian species the female lacks fully functional wings and is therefore flightless. She usually has a larger and heavier body than the male. It is common for her to devour the male during courtship or after mating.

The eggs of the Large Brown Mantis, *Archimantis latisyla* are laid in a frothy secretion which dries to form a firm, spongy case known as an ootheca. This is attached to part of a plant or to a flat surface such as a tree trunk or a rock. An ootheca can contain up to around four hundred eggs. The young hatch as small nymphs and their diet consists of small, soft-bodied insects such as aphids and thrips.

Members of this insect group occur in many areas of the world and tropical mantids can grow as long as 20 cm, eating creatures such as young birds, frogs and lizards, as well as insects.

Beetles

Over 350 000 different beetles inhabit our world. They have adapted to environments ranging from the polar regions to the hottest and wettest of the tropics. Australia has approximately 20 000 beetle species belonging to twenty-nine different families; this represents about one-third of the total number of insect species in this country.

Our beetle population is tremendously diverse. Some of the most colourful members are the Jewel Beetles (Bupestrids), which glisten with an iridescent brilliance. Other beetles dwell in ponds: the adult Water Beetle is well adapted to aquatic life with its boat-shaped body and flipper-like legs. Water beetles are also capable of spending time out of water. They are carnivorous and their food intake covers all forms of aquatic life.

Many of us may not have much of a fascination for beetles because we have come to know some through the damage they do to crops, or when weevils breed in our rolled oats, flour or other food. However, a large number of beetles are extremely useful to the gardener as they help to break down organic matter and aerate the soils. Others such as the introduced Dung Beetle (also called the Dor-beetle) roll dung into pellet-like shapes and take them down into the soil. Eggs are laid in the dung so that the newly hatched larvae have a ready-made food supply. Plants can also take up nutrients released by the dung. The diet of dung beetles is wide-ranging and can include both live and dead material.

In nature some beetles are vitally important for the pollination of Australian flowering plants, especially of *Angophora*, *Eucalyptus* and *Leptospermum* species, all of which are members of the Myrtle family.

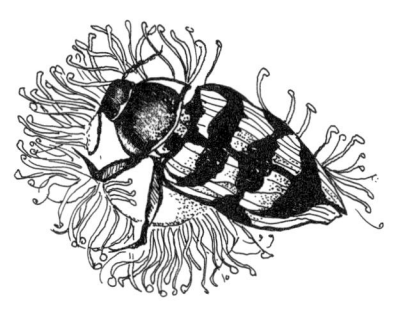

Jewel beetle

Ladybird beetles

Ladybirds are popular garden insects chiefly because their diet, in both the adult beetle and larval stages, includes pests such as aphids, mealy bugs, mites, scale, thrip and whiteflies. A ladybird beetle can eat up to around one hundred aphids in a day. Upon finding a plentiful supply of food the ladybird beetle will not only feed enthusiastically but also lay its small yellow eggs on the underside of a nearby leaf. As they hatch the larvae have their own food source immediately on hand.

There are many species of ladybirds. You can recognise them as small, rounded beetles in colours ranging from yellow to orange, reddish brown, blue, green or black. They commonly have two, four, six or seven prominent spots or blotches on the wing covers. A small group of ladybirds are in a separate insect group, including the twenty-eight-spot Ladybird, *Epilachna 28-punctata*. In addition to its greater number of spots this ladybird differs in its eating habits. It is a leaf-eater.

Ladybird pest control

The Australian Verdalia Ladybird, *Rodolia cardinalis*, was one of the first species used in biological pest control. It was taken to California in 1888 where it successfully controlled an outbreak of cottony cushion scale which had been devastating citrus orchards there. Another Australian species has subsequently been used in the USA in the control of mealy bugs. The ladybird larvae imitate the appearance of the bugs on which they feed.

Bees

The European or Italian Honey Bee was introduced in the early days of white settlement. This species has taken the rich and varied honey flora of Australia under its control. Alas, the poor native bees, many of which are smaller and less aggressive, have suffered from the interference of the European species.

Scientific studies have shown that the introduced honey-bee, in many cases, bypasses the pollination process. This affects plants such as *Callistemon* species (Bottlebrushes). The honey-bee may only touch the stigma (pollen

European wasps

The much-dreaded European Wasp is becoming well-entrenched in Australia. It has the superficial appearance of the introduced honey-bee but is longer and has bright yellow stripes. Colonies of this wasp should be reported to your local authority as soon as they are detected.

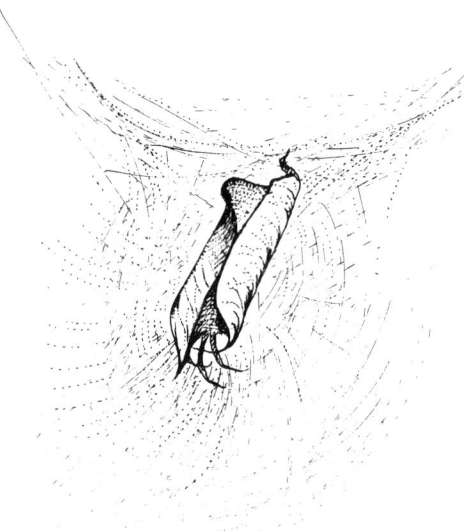
Leaf curl spider

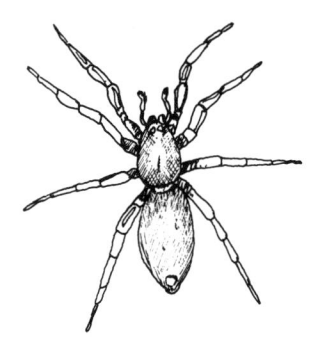
White-tailed spider

receiver) on less than 5 per cent of its visits to flowers while at the same time removing around 90 per cent of the nectar and pollen. Many of our native plants are pollinated by native bees but these plants and the native bees may 'miss out' if the European bee gets there first.

Native Australian bees placed in the genus *Trigona* are fairly common in the northern half of the continent and produce lovely honey. They don't establish large hives like those of the imported bee; rather, they tend to build their hives in small hollows of tree branches. Most native bees are non-social, solitary practitioners: the female may burrow into soil to lay one egg per burrow; others make a nest from cut leaf pieces. *Xylocopa bryorum*, one of the largest Australian bees reaches about 2.5cm in length and is known as the Large Carpenter Bee. It has a brilliant black abdomen and an orange hairy thorax. The Carpenter Bee bores into plant stems, where it lays eggs in bee-bread (honey and pollen mixture) thus guaranteeing food for the larvae.

Wasps

Wasps are usually readily distinguished from bees by their most slender waists. They do not seem to need much encouragement to visit gardens and it is fairly common to see and hear wasps building mud nests during the summer months. It can be somewhat disconcerting to open a door or window, which has not been opened since last summer, only to be showered with a mixture of dried mud and mummified insects.

Wasps come in a wide size range, from minute species to sizeable, attractive hornets, and they are all very valuable for controlling populations of many other insects. The small Brachinid, Chalcoid and Ichneumon Wasps are active in parasitising many plant pests by penetrating a large range of insects such as caterpillars, mites, scales, thrips and whitefly and laying their eggs inside them. The larger wasps directly attack caterpillars, cicadas and other grubs. They can let you know in no uncertain terms that it is best to let them be rather than to interfere with their activities.

Paperwasps from warmer climes can produce amazingly decorative nests, and you can spend many a pleasant hour observing their methods of gathering materials and nest construction.

Spiders

While some people have a sense of repulsion and even fear at the sight or touch of a spider, these creatures play an integral part in the balance of nature, both in bush areas and in home gardens. A spider's diet consists primarily of insects. They trap and hunt mainly at night and are sure to reduce your fly and mosquito populations!

Moving through the food chain we find that large numbers of spiders and their eggs are eaten by birds; they also contribute to the diet of lizards and frogs. Wasps often parasitise spider egg-sacs, laying their eggs in the sacs where young can hatch and enjoy a plentiful supply of food. Some species of wasps also parasitise adult spiders.

Spiders are members of the Arachnid family and are closely related to ticks and mites. They have eight legs and two body parts; insects (including beetles) have six legs and three body segments. Spiders can be categorised into many groups — some of the most common groups are: leaf spiders, house spiders, orb-web spiders, wolf spiders, water spiders, jumping spiders, money spiders, hunting spiders and trapdoor spiders.

There are over 1500 different species of spider in Australia, with only 20–30 posing any known major danger to humans. It should be pointed out that nearly all spiders produce small amounts of venom used for killing their prey. They should be treated with caution and not interfered with or handled unnecessarily. Some people may feel that webs are unsightly on buildings or in plant foliage and you may suffer some slight inconvenience if you walk into the odd strand stretched across a pathway. Remember that birds in your neighbourhood will find the spider webs a boon for their nest-making activities!

In general, there are many spiders which are present in our gardens but rarely seen. They have an uncanny knack of finding the perfect spot to trap their dinner. Some are very secretive and shy, hiding between leaves; others such as the Golden Orb are bold as brass, with their long, strong threads spanning large distances, supporting the architectural splendour of a central web which is sure to enmesh many an unsuspecting insect.

While some spiders are extremely small others can be 6cm or more in length. The largest Australian species are in the group commonly known as Birdeating Spiders. Their diet includes creatures such as small frogs, lizards, mice and birds. They are ground-dwelling species and live in burrows or constructed traps rather than aerial webs.

Some people may be surprised to discover that not all spiders are black, hairy, ugly creatures. There are red, green, white, striped, spotted and jewelled spiders; some of which are marvellously beautiful. Certain species are skilled in camouflage using bark, leaves or other aspects of their environment and, of course, many spiders display extraordinary webmaking craft.

Spider sense

Very few people other than keen enthusiasts ever seek actively to encourage spiders into their gardens. Most of us simply accept spiders as part of the total environment and are happy for them to occupy their own important niche in our gardens as long as they do not impinge on our living space! It is not necessary for us to rush for a large stick or insecticide spray every time we see a spider. We may wish to eliminate some in areas where young children play. The majority will cause us no harm at all and they certainly eat their share of insect pests. They are important allies!

Earthworms

The earthworm is one of nature's major garden helpers, working tirelessly in the area of soil improvement. Earthworms feed mainly on fallen leaves, dead grasses and other vegetable matter. They burrow down, aerating and cultivating the soil, digesting earth and organic matter as they go.

Worms have a muscular gizzard where their food is finely ground. The material then enters the intestine where it is digested by enzymes before being excreted as castings. Worm castings are noted for their high plant nutrient value because they contain humus, nitrogen, phosphorus and potassium and trace elements. Castings can be purchased as a means of soil enrichment. They are highly prized by enthusiastic organic gardeners.

There are hundreds of different earthworm species throughout the world, including many which are native in Australia. Most of the worms we see in our gardens are, however, of European origin. Possibly the most unusual Australian species is the giant earthworm from South Gippsland in Victoria, which can grow to around 3m long. All earthworms are bisexual. Each is capable of laying an egg capsule after first being fertilised by another worm.

Earthworms can form burrows in the soil to a depth of 1 m or more. The value of earthworms in the garden can be multiplied by deliberately designing compost heaps or bins to foster their activities and breeding. A compost heap suitable for worms should have a high content of animal manure and be both dark and moist around the edges and on top of the heap. Worms are active only in slow-composting areas, with a temperature no greater than 25° Celsius.

In addition to their own value in the garden worms also provide a natural food source for other creatures such as birds, lizards and frogs. Earthworms can also act as an indicator of soil quality. They dislike soils which are strongly alkaline or too acidic so are rarely found in such conditions. Soils must also contain organic matter for earthworms to thrive.

Excessive worm activity can in some situations be undesirable, particularly with container-grown plants if potting mix is carried out of the

On a misty, moist morning, you may come across a beautiful dew-covered web.

Earthworms have a head and a tail, but no eyes. If a worm is cut in half it will not, as some of us may think, grow into two separate worms. The head can grow a new tail but the cut-off tail is not able to grow a new head.

Compost bins specifically designed to encourage worm activity are available commercially. Worm farming is becoming increasingly recognised for its high value to the home gardener.

container or when worm castings cause drainage holes to become blocked. Plants can be re-potted to eliminate the worms or an application of a complete garden fertiliser usually does the trick. Chemical pesticides are not recommended as they can be readily transferred through the food chain.

Crickets and grasshoppers

Crickets and grasshoppers are closely related and common throughout Australia. Field crickets and grasshoppers are avid chewers of leaves and twigs and can do inestimable damage if they are in plague proportions but in general they don't pose serious problems for gardeners. Hopefully your bird population will be large enough to keep them under control.

Sometimes you may wonder what has been chewing on soft new growth when you are sure it is not an earwig. Field crickets may be the culprits as they are night operators. The chirping or stridulation of crickets is commonplace during summer evenings and is created by males rubbing their wings together.

On the other hand, tree crickets, also known as long-horned grasshoppers because of their extremely long and slender antennae, are sometimes predators of insect caterpillars and eggs, which somewhat makes up for their tendency to chew soft leaves. When in their nymph form, tree crickets often reside in leaves bound together in the upper canopy but as they mature they can be found at lower levels using crevices beneath bark for protection.

Cicadas

We only seem to remember cicadas each summer from year to year because we immediately recognise their call. The noise is produced by the males as they try to entice a female to mate. This calling is often referred to as singing but as insects don't have voice boxes they have to use other means of sound production. Male cicadas have a cavernous abdominal cavity and at the underside junction of the abdomen and thorax there are two 'drums', inside which are tightly stretched membranes activated by muscles.

Cicadas usually hatch in autumn from eggs which were deposited by the female in slits in the bark of trees. The nymphs drop to the ground and begin their big tunnelling adventure underground where they can spend many years. Nymphs feed through a sharply pointed proboscis that penetrates roots and draws out plant sap. The nymph emerges in early summer to renew the life cycle once more. These insects do not pose a serious threat to plants as the damage caused by their sap-sucking is minimal.

Many birds, lizards, spiders, small marsupials such as Sugar Gliders, as well as predatory insects help to control the proliferation of cicadas.

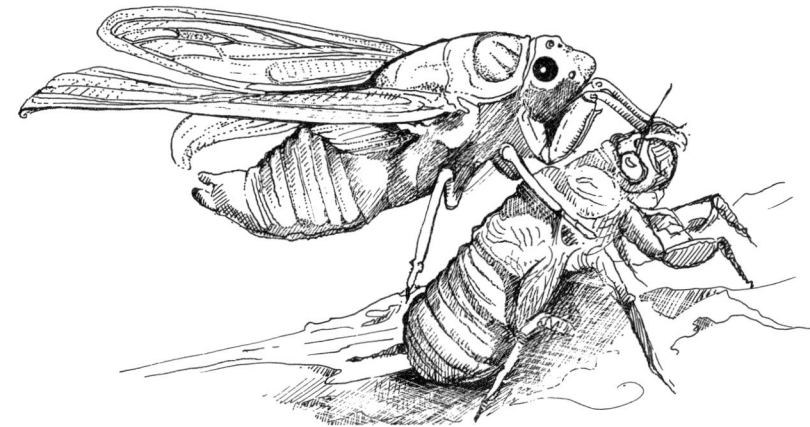

The shell of a nymph cicada splits to allow the winged adult cicada to emerge.

Mammals, reptiles, amphibians and fish

Mammals

Mammals are animals which can maintain their warm body temperature at a reasonably constant level; their skin is hairy (to varying degrees); and the young are fed milk secreted from the mammary glands of females. Possums, koalas, bandicoots, echidnas, bush rats, native mice and bats are all mammals.

Possums

When the word 'possum' is mentioned an animated conversation about the happenings on the roof or in the ceiling usually follows. However, there is more to the possum world than the bounding, crashing, rambunctious Brush-tailed Possum — the bane of so many people's evenings.

The exquisite and delightful Ring-tailed Possum is easily distinguished from its brush-tailed relative by its smaller size and slender white-tipped tail, which it uses as an extra 'hand' in moving from plant to plant. Ring-tails may cause havoc among your favourite rose blooms but they rarely do substantial damage. They are very good at pruning shrubs and trees.

Ring-tailed and brush-tailed possums may become very tame if people are constantly active near their nests, and especially if food such as ripe fruit is provided for them regularly. Possums love to feast upon the new growth of plants so it could prove beneficial for some of your well-loved plants if an alternative source of foliage is available. So why not try and provide this service by growing some eucalypts which respond very well to regular coppicing; some examples are, *Eucalyptus cinerea*, *E. crenulata*, *E. pulverulenta*, *E. radiata* and *E. cephalocarpa*. In our garden we removed at about ground level the trunk of a very sickly Long-leaved Box, *E. goniocalyx* and since the new juvenile growth has emerged it has been the regular 'dining joint' for some of the local posssums.

Other small members of the possum family such as pigmy possums and the various gliders (Feathertail, Sugar, Squirrel and Greater Glider) are exciting to observe but unless your property has, or adjoins, extensive bushland or is near a large tract of continuous forest or woodland, it is unlikely that they will be present in the area. The small possums and gliders rely on nectar from flowers, sweet exudation from branches, leaves, insects and to a lesser degree the squirrel glider will also eat birds and small animals.

Ring-tailed possums prefer to nest in hollow branches or dense foliage. Bushy climbers, trees and shrubs are all beneficial. Species of *Kennedia*, *Pandorea*, *Acmena*, *Syzygium*, *Melaleuca* are popular sites for nest building.

Ring-tailed Possum in a nest.

Koala food

Koalas have a very specialised diet — they eat leaves from only a limited range of eucalypts, plus one or two other species.

Eucalyptus botryoides ssp. *botryoides* and ssp. *saligna*
  E. camaldulensis
  E. drepanophylla
  E. globulus
  E. goniocalyx
  E. grandis
  E. haemastoma
  E. maculata
  E. melliodora
  E. microcarpa
  E. microcorys
  E. moluccana
  E. nicholii
  E. obliqua
  E. ovata
  E. paniculata
  E. pilularis
  E. polyanthemos
  E. propinqua
  E. pryoriana
  E. punctata
  E. racemosa
  E. radiata
  E. regnans
  E. resinifera
  E. robusta
  E. rubida
  E. tereticornis
  E. viminalis
Lophostemon confertus

If you wish to attract possums and there is a shortage of nesting hollows then provision can be made by using artificial nesting hollows or boxes. The boxes should have an opening of less than 7 cm diameter because this dimension excludes the brush-tailed possum. Nest boxes can be placed as high as possible in trees, but where they can be reached by ladder or other means if maintenance is required.

Brush-tailed possums are not usually regarded as loveable creatures, particularly when they helter-skelter along rooftops at night time. However, there are some options that can lead to more peaceful nights! Firstly, you can provide a resting or nesting place for the possum during the day by placing an artificial nesting hollow with a 12 cm opening on a nearby tree. Also, make sure that after the possum leaves the house roof during the night all entries to the roof are blocked to prevent re-entry.

Cage-type possum traps are available from many municipalities and these can be used to capture a possum before re-locating it away from your property. Remember that a possum can travel large distances to return to its former territory and in the event of that territory remaining vacant it is highly likely that another possum will move in! Setting up a nesting box which allows peaceful coexistence for both humans and the odd possum is the most desirable solution.

Koalas

Many gardeners dream of having a visit from a koala but, again, unless your garden is close to forest or bushland already inhabited by koalas, it will be a rare occurrence to have visits from them. The distribution range of koalas extends over eastern Queensland, eastern New South Wales and Victoria with introduced populations in South Australia (including Kangaroo Island) and Western Australia. Visiting koalas will stay only for short periods, usually one to five days. Koalas need and devour large amounts of foliage and they usually move to another location during the night.

If you wish to attract koalas please realise that although they may look like nice, cuddly, quiet bundles of fluff in zoos and sanctuaries, their night activities often become a frenzied and very noisy affair, especially during the mating season.

Bandicoots

These quaint marsupials with very functional, long-pointed noses are found in a variety of habitats including woodlands which have a thick understorey of grass tussocks. In some areas bandicoots have adapted fairly well to the encroachment of suburbia, except that they do not appreciate the blockades of fences at ground level which are usually built on new subdivisions.

You may have noticed cone-shaped holes in your garden or lawn. These are almost certainly the result of bandicoots seeking root-chomping grubs and other insect larvae, weevils, or the odd earthworm. Their diet also includes spiders, roots and other vegetable matter.

It is very hard to attract bandicoots as they usually have a wide-wandering range. They love to make a nest of dried grass in a hollow amongst dense tussock vegetation. Usually bandicoots forage as individuals and you may observe them in the twilight or during the night. If you hear sneezes coming from the undergrowth it is a fair indication that you are privileged to have bandicoots! Dogs and cats can be very bothersome for bandicoots, especially when they are very young.

Phascolarctos cinereus (Koala)

Echidnas (spiny anteaters)

What excitement ensues when one of these captivating creatures visits your garden! You'll need to have plenty of ant or termite nests for this egg-laying mammal to be a regular visitor. Echidnas (along with one- and two-year old humans) enjoy chewing on sand and dirt; in fact, they devour large portions of earth all their life.

Only a few gardeners who live close to bushland are likely to experience an echidna in their garden. Echidnas occur over a very widespread range in Australia and usually prefer a habitat which has fairly dense lower vegetation of shrubs and tussocks and lots of ant nests. They are very sensitive to the vibrations of pounding feet and will quickly bury themselves, often leaving their quills or spines exposed as protection against predators.

Echidna

Bush rats

Fancy wanting rats or mice to come into the garden! You may be surprised to learn that in Australia we do have quite a number of interesting and even very attractive native rodents. Unfortunately, native rats are often lumped together with the infamous introduced Ship Rat, *Rattus rattus* or the Brown Rat, *Rattus norvegicus*. These rats are rarely encountered in bush areas so your efforts to eradicate introduced rats by using commercial baits may also have a detrimental effect on the populations of your own native rats.

Some common Australian rats

It is valuable to be able to identify the rats in your area.

Bush Rat — has a short snout, short ears and light brown fur on its upperparts, while underneath it is greyish-buff with white hairs on its feet. Occurs in Queensland, New South Wales, Victoria, south-eastern South Australia and Western Australia. Usually little evidence of its runways. Lives under fallen logs and branches and has small burrows to about 3 m long with a grass-lined nest at the end.

Swamp Rat — has yellowish-brown to blackish-brown long soft fur above and an undersurface of greyish to yellow grey fur. Its ears are small. Has prominent runways and deep burrows in dry places but nests in tussocks in wet areas. Found in New South Wales, Victoria, south-eastern South Australia, Tasmania and Bass Strait Islands.

Broad-toothed Rat — is distinguished by its rounded ears and very short snout. Builds its nest of shredded material in a sedge or grass tussock. Found in south-eastern New South Wales, Victoria and Tasmania.

Water Rat — has a flattened head and large feet. Its tail is thickened at the base then tapers to its end. This distinctive rat inhabitats estuaries and inland waterways and feeds mainly on mussels, frogs, fish, snails and yabbies.

Native rats like to have plenty of vegetation at ground level through which they make their runs. They may be found in forests, woodlands and heathlands and their diet consists of grass stems and roots, fungi, flowers, leaves, seeds, insects and insect larvae and worms.

Bush rat

Introduced rats

Rattus rattus — is variable in colour. It can be black with dark grey beneath, or brown with cream or light to dark grey beneath. The head is slender with a pointed snout and large ears. Its tail is as long or longer than the body. Usually not found in dry regions.

Rattus norvegicus — is greyish to tan-brown with white to pale grey beneath. Its snout is large and blunt, ears are short as is the tail. Occurs in coastal cities and towns.

Native mice

Native mice are rarely encountered in suburban areas but some gardeners may be privileged to have some native marsupial mice, *Antechinus* species as residents or visitors. Antechinus have a narrow elongated nose, short broad ears and usually large eyes. These fascinating creatures live a very frantic and short life. They reach sexual maturity within their first year and after mating — a rather rigorous and drawn out affair, especially for the Brown and Dusky Antechinus — the male usually dies while the female may sometimes last another season for breeding. Generally they are nocturnal animals but also may be seen in daylight. Insects, worms and small lizards form the basis of their diet. They make a nest of bark, grass and leaves in tussocks, hollow logs, rock crevices, wood piles or sometimes in bush litter.

The New Holland Mouse may be encountered in gardens that are near bushland in south-eastern Australia. This nocturnal animal is usually found in recent regrowth areas as it likes dense vegetation. It is similar to the House Mouse but has a heavier build. The New Holland Mouse makes its nest at the base of a tussock. Other native mice such as the Smokey Mouse, Brown Desert Mouse and the various Hopping Mice are only likely to be seen away from urban areas with the latter usually confined to semi-arid or arid regions.

The introduced House or Domestic Mouse has long membranous ears and is attracted to buildings and compost areas in particular. Principally it is a seed-eater but also enjoys virtually any household food. The nest is made with shredded matter and paper is often used. Nests can be found in buildings as well as a range of locations which provide security; they sometimes also make burrows in paddocks or grassland. Domestic mice plagues are an infrequent phenomenon which usually occur when climatic factors provide good breeding conditions and this situation combined with an imbalance of predators to keep the numbers under control may lead to a population explosion.

Brown rat

Bats

Australia has a very large population of these highly developed flying mammals. Bats are the only mammals which fly! Their means of navigation in the dark of night by echo-locating is marvellous. They emit very high pitched sounds which bounce back from objects allowing them to proceed without obstruction.

Some people are petrified by bats because of the mythology of vampires; others dismiss them as unimportant. They are a fascinating group of animals and probably most of us are unaware of their presence in our gardens, unless we are visited by the chattering and somewhat odorous fruit bats.

Bats are divided into two categories. The fruit or blossom-eating group are generally larger than other bats. They have long faces and lack tails. In most cases they are arboreal and rest in mangroves, trees or palms before taking off at dusk and returning before dawn. It is such a pity these bats have been burdened with the tag of flying-foxes as they are not even closely related to foxes. Fruit bats eat native plant fruits as well as those of some introduced plants. They also thrive on prolific nectar and pollen-producing flowers, with eucalypts and melaleucas among the most popular.

The second group of bats are insectivorous bats. They are much smaller than the fruit bats and are distinguished by having tails and short faces. These

Australia's more common bats

Fruit bats
- Red Flying-fox
- Black Flying-fox
- Grey-headed Flying-fox
- Queensland Blossom Bat

Insectivorous bats
- Lesser Long-eared Bat
- Greater Long-eared Bat
- Chocolate Bat
- Little Brown Bat
- Little Flat Bat
- Gould's Wattled Bat
- White-striped Bat

The huge flower-heads of *Doryanthes palmeri* attract honeyeaters. These birds sometimes become intoxicated if the flower nectar has fermented. In the foreground are a couple of spiky yuccas from the Americas.

In late spring you'll often see the Spotted Skipper Butterfly visiting the Woolly Tea-tree, *Leptospermum lanigerum* to gather nectar.

This open, sunny site is covered in late summer/early autumn flowers. You can see orange-flowered bottlebrush, *Beaufortia sparsa* which will tempt honeyeaters, while the yellow, *Chrysocephalum apiculatum* and mauve and blue scaevolas will attract butterflies and other insects.

Water plays a vital role in creating wildlife habitat. In this scene, the poolside vegetation will be crawling with snacks for these visiting Pacific Black ducks. Migratory ducks may return to the same nesting site each year. (PHOTO: BILL KING)

Two recently emerged Imperial White Butterflies. You can see a discarded chrysalis on the twig between the butterflies. This butterfly is called the Imperial White because the upper surface of its wings, not visible in this picture, is mainly white. In a few hours, the butterflies will be strong enough to open their wings and fly off.

One of the most common tree frogs is Ewings Tree-frog. They are more active in the evenings chasing after insects and mosquitoes. This frog is pictured resting on a leaf of Cunjevoi, *Alocasia macrorrhizos*, which has pleasantly perfumed, greenish-yellow, hood-shaped flowers.

Brown Thornbills often build their glorious grassy nests near ground level and therefore are easy prey to cats and other predators. Blue wrens also build close to ground level. (PHOTO: BILL KING)

This small, clay-based pool provides an excellent wildlife habitat as well as some beautiful reflections. Many water-loving plants are growing around the margins, including: in the patch of sunlight, the light green, fine-foliaged *Myriophyllum variifolium*; the clover-like foliage of Common Nardoo, *Marsilea drummondii*; and various grasses and rushes.

bats are extremely important in the control insect populations. Most insectivorous bats gather their food on the wing, although the Lesser Long-eared Bat often lands on the ground to capture creatures such as beetles. These bats, being small, can often squeeze through small openings in order to gain shelter for the day. A number of species will lodge in wall cavities, house eaves, house or shed roofs, but do not usually cause any damage. They commonly use tree hollows, cavities underneath bark, cracks in farm fenceposts or in timber stacks, and on occasions are known to frequent unattended clothes hanging in sheds. Abandoned nests of Fairy Martin birds are a favourite with some bats. Caves and mining shafts are also common haunts of insectivorous bats.

If you would like to have bats as residents, bat nesting boxes can be installed in trees or on the sides of houses. They are best situated at least 3m above the ground. It could also be worth experimenting with some castoff farm fenceposts if they are full of crevices.

Lesser Long-eared Bats are known to move from roosting sites very regularly; it can be as often as every day. The moral of this tale is to have a large number of suitable roosts!

Grey-headed Flying Fox

Lizards

Australia has a very rich and diverse population of native lizards, tortoises, turtles, snakes and crocodiles. While home gardeners are unlikely to have any wish to encourage the latter to take up residence amongst their favourite plants, there are numerous lizards that most of us would happily have around.

A lizard's diet consists mainly of slugs, snails, insects, spiders, centipedes, scorpions and other small creatures which inhabit leaf litter or garden understorey layers near ground level. Hence the need for plenty of mulch, low spreading plants and tussocks. The availability of permanent water is important in encouraging lizards to remain within any particular area. These reptiles are very useful for garden pest control. Some species also enjoy fleshy plant fruits and nectar-rich flowers. Larger lizard species have no qualms about consuming some of their smaller relatives, so it is fortunate that smaller lizards usually produce a greater number of offspring to offset this predation.

The smaller species of lizards usually find their own way into a garden, and live there happily provided they are not eliminated by pesticides, snail baits or from predation by cats and dogs. They do have the wonderful capacity to grow a new tail if it is lost along the way.

There are over 250 Australian lizards varying in size from tiny skinks and geckos a few centimetres long to the large goannas or monitor lizards. Australia's largest lizard is the Perentie Monitor (*Varanus giganteus*) which commonly grows around 1.5m long but can reach 2.5m or more. It lives in arid inland regions.

Skink lizards

The skink family has made the most successful adaptation to Australia's climate, geology and vegetation. Blue-tongues and shinglebacks are among the best known of Australian lizards but most people do not realise that they are members of this large category of lizards.

Skinks are distinguished from other lizards by their wedge-shaped heads, streamlined and elongated bodies. Their tongues are usually notched at the tip and they have small limbs. Often they are slender, shiny, and beautifully marked reptiles. Skinks, like other reptiles, are cold-blooded and hibernate during cold months. They are most active during the day. They have a voracious appetite for snails, slugs, moths, beetles and flies, and are therefore of immense benefit if present in our gardens. Most skinks are carnivorous but quite a number eat vegetation. Blotched blue-tongue lizards have a whopping appetite for soft-petalled flowers and fleshy native fruits. They will also enjoy cultivated strawberries. So watch out! And they can be quick enough to catch the odd fly now and again.

Shinglebacks help control the population of potential garden pests such as snails and slugs.

Regulations govern the keeping of reptiles in captivity in Australia, so advice on this aspect should be sought if you are wishing to enclose an area in your garden. An outside area open to the elements is recommended unless keeping species from areas with different climatic conditions to that which prevail in your region.

Perhaps you have come across a Stumpy-tail, also known as the Shingleback, in its characteristic defensive pose, with its big open mouth and bluish tongue, sometimes camouflaged by grass leaves and other vegetation. Skinks love to soak up the sun's rays and often do this on suitably sited rocks or logs. Most skinks produce young by laying soft-shelled eggs. The eggs need to be in areas of constant humidity — leaf litter or friable loose soil or gravel is well-suited to this purpose. The larger skinks such as blue-tongues are the only lizards that produce live young. The babies have an attached egg-sac which is their initial food source after birth.

Geckos

Soft-skinned Geckos are found throughout Australia and are closely related to skinks. They are nocturnal animals and seek refuge beneath rocks, loose bark and in hollow logs during the day. Some may even burrow in loose sandy soil.

Most geckos are insectivorous, although some of the larger species, such as the Central Knob-tailed Gecko from Central Australia, eat small skinks and geckos. Like most lizards, geckos lay eggs in sheltered sites.

Legless lizards

Legless lizards are not likely to be found in many gardens unless there is plenty of bushland or maybe a cemetery or two nearby. Neglected cemeteries are often excellent refuges for some of our smaller wildlife. Some legless lizards are now among the rarest of Australian reptiles.

Legless lizards can be misidentified as snakes but on closer inspection you'll notice that while snakes have forked tongues, the tongue of a legless lizard is broad. These lizards are also valuable for controlling insect populations and will eat small skinks and geckos. They prefer a habitat with rocks, logs and tufting grasses.

Dragon lizards

The dragon lizard species are wonderful animals rarely seen in gardens unless, as for the legless lizards, there is bushland close by. To have the Common Bearded Dragon or Eastern Water Dragon or any other native dragon on your property would be a delight. Dragon lizards have a vigorous and sensational courting display.

Snakes

Many people seem to have an inherent fear of these creatures, combined with the dilemma of what to do when they see a long slender body slithering through the grass or shrubbery.

Certainly, many snakes are poisonous and should not be approached closely or touched unless you are an experienced snake-handler. People are more likely to be bitten during their so-called acts of bravery rather than by a threatened snake which has been inadvertently trodden on due to its magnificent camouflage or our lack of concentration. You must be extremely attentive after dark as this is when snakes are mostly active.

There are some marvellous small snakes; their diet consisting of ants and other small creatures. Although venomous, they don't pose any real danger to humans because of their very small jaws. These species include the White-lipped Snake of eastern NSW, Victoria and Tasmania, Collared Whip Snake from Queensland and Northern Territory and the Red-naped Snake from the northern two-thirds of Australia. Snakes along with lizards are protected animals and therefore it is illegal to kill them.

Frogs

Much has been said and written about the current decline in frog numbers in Australia. It is also a worldwide phenomenon. Frogs are regarded as one of the best indicators of the general ecological wellbeing and balance in an area and the absence of frogs where previously they have been plentiful is being viewed with concern by those involved in ecological studies and management. Scientists have not identified the cause of this widespread trend. Frogs have been on this earth for about 350 million years. Dinosaurs were around for less than one-third of that time.

Studies are currently underway and you can be part of these studies by becoming involved with *Frogwatch*. *Frogwatch* members identify frog calls and observe frog habitats and contribute these records to a large database. For further details on *Frogwatch* contact state government conservation departments.

There are over 2000 different frog species throughout the world. This includes the creatures commonly known as toads. The term 'toad' is usually applied to slow-moving species which have dark, warty skin and which are generally considered unattractive. A frog has smoother skin; is an avid jumper; often an active climber and is generally viewed more favourably. This distinction is reinforced in children's books where frogs are frequently coloured bright green or golden (as they often are in nature). Anyway, who has ever heard of eating a chocolate toad?

One member of the true toad family is the Cane Toad, *Bufo marinus*, introduced in 1935 to control pests in sugar canefields. Alas, this form of biological control failed and now the Cane Toad is a serious pest in northern Australia and should be eradicated, if possible!

Frogs undergo an amazing metamorphosis. After hatching from small eggs laid in a jelly-like substance, most frogs begin their life as water-dwelling tadpoles feeding on green algae and minute forms of aquatic life (some tadpoles start life in moist soils and never live in water). As they develop lungs and four legs they leave the water and their diet changes to include a smorgasbord of flies, mosquitoes and other small creatures. Most frogs capture these with the aid of their long tongue which they can flick out with a very quick, sharp movement, catching the insect with the tip.

Australia and New Guinea have many frog species not found elsewhere in the world. They include tree frogs, ground-dwellers and some which are found in a wide variety of moist habitats. In the garden, frogs will help to reduce the number of mosquitoes in and around pools or other water-holding locations. Their diet also includes slugs, snails, spiders, mites, a wide range of insects, worms and small lizards and even other smaller frogs. Frogs vary considerably in size, and the larger the frog the more food it eats. Most of their foraging is done at night time.

Frogs contribute to the food chain: their eggs are food for fish and for this reason sometimes it can be difficult to have frogs and fish in the same pool. One way to overcome this problem is to have separate pools for fish and frogs, provided you have sufficient space. Ants are sometimes predators of frog's eggs. Tadpoles are eagerly sought by a large range of aquatic insects, spiders, turtles, snakes, birds and rats to name but a few; while snakes and birds are the major predators of adult frogs.

Frogs communicate with each other through a range of different and distinctive calling notes. These can vary from a low croaking to a high pitched scream-like call. It is only male frogs that call and it is a strategy to entice females during the breeding season as well as for territorial reasons. Some people find these calls as interesting and appealing as bird calls but, if a pond

The Pobblebonk or Banjo Frog frequents permanent or temporary swamps and waterways and the surrounding areas. Its distinctive call, 'bonk' is often repeated in quick succession. (PHOTO: BILL KING)

Tortoises and turtles

When is a tortoise a turtle and vice versa? Usually, the term 'turtle' is applied to larger, sea-going creatures and 'tortoise' refers to land inhabitants. Turtles have flippers and tortoises have clawed feet.

Tortoises are long-lived creatures that hibernate during the cold months. They may be irregular visitors to gardens that adjoin bushland and have a permanent freshwater pool. A good supply of their favourite foods including snails, fish, frogs and yabbies will encourage them to stay. Breeding tortoises will need to have access to sandy soil in which to lay their eggs.

The Eastern Snake-necked Turtle, also called the Long-necked Tortoise, has a wide distribution extending from north-eastern Queensland to south-eastern Australia.

is close to the house, particularly the bedrooms, the noise may not be appreciated as much. Some find it soothing, but others consider it makes sleep difficult. Usually time heals any inconvenience!

If you wish to encourage frogs to your garden it is important to have at least one pool which always contains water. This will provide the habitat required for reproduction for most frogs and also the environment to encourage the creatures which are their major food supply. Mossy sheltered hollows or a moist ferny area are an excellent addition. Another possibility is to scoop out hollows to form temporary, shallow pools. It is a common occurrence for precious rainwater to flow over and down our properties only to end up in gutters and drains; you can overcome this waste of water by digging out the topsoil in areas which are natural drainage lines. Pools such as these can be excellent habitat for frogs if they have vegetation and foliage litter. A side benefit is that the water slowly penetrates the soil and is a valuable method of providing a deep soaking for plants.

All pools need camouflage to protect frogs from their predators. Some frogs prefer areas of dense planting extending down to ground level; others warmly appreciate a piece of matting or hessian on the ground — but of course we can't really say that of these 'cold-blooded' creatures. The use of suitable plants in and around pools is paramount if you wish to have an array of frogs in your garden. (See plant lists; Chapter 1, pages 7–8.)

Once you have these prerequisites you should have an influx of frogs as they are excellent at locating preferred habitat and they will do the rest and hopefully provide you with much pleasure.

Fish

We would all agree it is extremely difficult to *attract* fish to a garden. However, if you have a pool, then you can certainly stock it with fish and they may even continue to live and breed there — if suitable fish are selected and the habitat is adequate for their needs. What very frequently happens is that the ubiquitous goldfish, members of the notorious carp family, often end up becoming the sole inhabitants.

There are other options and one often quoted recommendation is to put in some mosquito fish because they eat mosquito 'wrigglers'. This can lead to problems because mosquito fish are inveterate nibblers of the fins of other fish and consequently will dominate pond life. So keep away from mosquito fish! I can speak from experience when some were inadvertently introduced to one of our pools.

Native fish are just as efficient at controlling mosquito larvae. If you are able to procure the rarely procurable Native Pygmy Perch, you'll find they are excellent insect controllers, and will breed in the pool. Murray River Rainbowfish, *Melanolaenia fluviatilis* and *Galaxias olidus* would also be worth trying. Other small native fish such as the Common Jollytail, *Galaxias maculata* will live for a time in pools but will die out after a couple of years. These fish spawn on spring tides which carry the freshly laid eggs out to sea where they can hatch. Later the young fish will return to the rivers.

Other larger native fish such as Golden Perch, Silver Perch or Black Fish can be put in the pool with a view to catching them later for food if that is your desire. Trout can also be treated in the same manner. One word of warning, steer away from using fish such as carp in clay-based pool, you will never have a clear pool with them in residence.

Plants for wildlife gardens

This section provides descriptions of over 170 Australian plants. Various plant groups are represented including: annuals and other short-lived plants; grasses, lilies and tufting plants; groundcovers; climbers; ferns and fern allies; palms; shrubs and trees. Further information on these plants and many more can be found in other titles in this series, including *Gardening with Australian plants* and *Coastal gardening in Australia*.

Annuals and short-lived plants

Annuals are excellent for planting in new, young or recently renovated gardens where they will help to fill obvious gaps among the slower-growing groundcovers, tufts and clumps, shrubs and trees. Annuals can also be used for providing short-term visual accents in any desired area. The annual everlastings are excellent for attracting butterflies and other insects.

Actinotus helianthi
Flannel Flower

A somewhat woody small plant, about 0.5–1m x 0.5m, with deeply lobed, hairy, greyish-green leaves. The felty creamy-white, daisy-like flowers are produced over spring and summer. Tip prune when young and cut flowering stems for indoor decoration.

Bracteantha bracteata
(syn. *Helichrysum bracteatum*)
Everlastings; Strawflowers; Paper Daisies

There is a marvellous range of these colourful and floriferous plants offered by nurseries. All are exceptional for butterfly attraction.

Bracteantha bracteata

Flowers are white, cream, yellow, gold and pink. Plants respond well to regular pruning with an almost constant display of handsome papery daisies. Some cultivars to look out for are 'Cockatoo', 'Dargan Hill Monarch', 'Golden Bowerbird', 'Princess of Wales', 'Pink Swirls' and 'White Monarch'.

Code key

Light levels

☼ Light shade or semi-shade

● Full shade

☼ Sun

Temperature

🌡 Cool, frost tolerant to −4°C (parts of plants may be damaged)

🌡 Warm, best where minimum is 2°C (often tolerates light frosts)

Water requirements

◊◊ Moist, but well drained

◊ Withstands periods of dryness

◊◊ Tolerates wet or poorly drained conditions

Special features

🌸 Flower

◯ Fruit

↳ Perfume

🐦 Attracts nectar-feeding birds

🐦 Attracts insect-eating birds

🐦 Attracts seed and fruit-eating birds

🦋 Butterfly attracting

🌿 Refuge or nesting plant

Rhodanthe species
Everlastings; Sunrays

Rhodanthe chlorocephala ssp. *rosea* (syn. *Helipterum roseum*) and *R. manglesii* (syn. *Helipterum manglesii*) have lovely white to deep pink daisies in late winter and spring. Seed should be sown in autumn, directly into a sunny site with well-prepared friable soil.

Trachymene coerulea
Rottnest Daisy

A lovely tall-growing annual with much-divided leaves. In late spring and summer plants have mauve-blue semi-globular heads composed of many small flowers. Can be mass-planted or grown in scattered or informal drifts.

A White-faced Heron goes fishing among some rushes growing in shallow water.

Grasses, lilies and other tufting plants

A garden lacking plants of this type is incomplete. These plants provide an alternative accent to the foliage of groundcovers, shrubs and trees. The mood of a garden is changed marvellously by having plants with long, narrow foliage which waves at the whim of the wind.

As well as the grasses listed in this section there are many other grasses which are excellent plants for habitat gardens. *Microlaena stipoides* (Weeping Grass) has soft bright green leaves and weeping flower-heads, while *Themeda triandra* (Kangaroo Grass) is a welcome addition, especially in summer when it has bronze highlights.

A warning! I recommend only planting grasses which are native to your area — otherwise you may introduce a weed problem which could have far-reaching effects.

Alocasia macrorrhizos
Cunjevoi; Spoon Lily

A perennial herb with thick, fleshy leaf stalks and spreading, thin, green to dark green blades growing up to 1–2m in height. The pleasantly fragrant pale yellow or yellowish-green flowers are displayed over late spring to early autumn and often the glossy red fruits are borne in clusters. Ideal for growing among ferns.

Anigozanthos species and cultivars
Kangaroo Paws

Nurseries now stock a great variety of kangaroo paws, from dwarf tufts to vigorous clumps, in a kaleidoscope of flower colours. Some are more reliable than others in cultivation. For growing success, purchase plants which are least affected by blackening of leaves. Over late spring and summer, nectar-feeding birds will be constant visitors to flowering plants. Plants do best in friable soils.

Baumea articulata
Jointed Twig Rush

A moisture-loving herb with creeping roots and long, rush-like, dark green leaves. Over summer the drooping clusters of small brown flowers are prominent. Excellent for pool edges and bog gardens. It is a host plant for butterfly larvae as well as a nectar provider for butterflies.

Blandfordia grandiflora
Christmas Bells

Loose clusters of spectacular orange-red and yellow (or all yellow), flared waxy bells are produced during summer, at the ends of vertical stalks which arise from a sparse, grass-like clump of foliage. *Blandfordia nobilis* is similar but has narrower bells.

Carex fascicularis
Tassel Sedge

This tussocking sedge is usually 0.5–1m tall and has arching narrow green leaves. The pendent tassels are especially evident during spring and summer. Ideal for pool edge planting as a refuge for frogs and insects. Other *Carex* species are worth considering: *C. gaudichaudiana*, green to greyish foliage, forms a low-spreading tuft or mat; *C. inversa*, excellent for boggy spots.

Chionochloa pallida
Red-anther Wallaby Grass

A clumping grass with arching, fine leaves. The delicately composed flowers deserve close attention. Highly suited to semi-shaded dry sites.

Craspedia and *Pycnosorus* species
Billy Buttons; Drumsticks

All craspedias are ornamental when their globular to semi-globular flower-heads of cream, yellow-gold or orange are displayed. *P. globosus* (syn. *Craspedia globosa*) which has narrow silvery leaves does best in heavy soils and may reach 1m in height, while the other species prefer lighter, friable soils and are rarely more than 0.5m tall.

Crinum
Swamp Lily; River Lily

Crinums provide a bold, textural component to gardens. Their alluringly fragrant flowers are prominently displayed during spring to autumn. *C. pedunculatum* is the most adaptable of the Australian species, but *C. asiaticum* and *C. flaccidum* are worth trying too.

Dianella
Flax Lilies

Dianella tasmanica (Tasman Flax Lily) is a vigorous, spreading species which prefers a moist, sheltered site and grows well with ferns. The pale blue starry flowers give way to brilliant purplish blue berries. *D. revoluta* is very adaptable, as is *D. caerulea*, which has pale to dark blue flowers.

Dianella caerulea

Doryanthes

The broad, long leaves of doryanthes contrast markedly well with most other plants. The large red flowers produced in spring are tubular with flared lobes. They are arranged in flat-topped clusters on tall erect stalks in *D. excelsa*, while *D. palmeri* has long spreading (somewhat arching) flower-spikes. Plants may not flower every year.

Gahnia sieberiana
Red-fruited Sword-sedge

A large tussocking plant with long, sharp-edged, grass-like dark green leaves. Terminal panicles of cream flowers during spring and summer are followed by small brownish-red fruits. This is a host plant for Sword-grass Brown Butterfly larvae. All gahnias are excellent habitat plants but they are often difficult to procure. *G. melanocarpa*, *G. radula* and *G. trifida* are worth consideration.

Sword-grass Brown Butterfly

Isolepis
Club-rushes

The floating *I. fluitans* is a moisture-lover with narrow, pale green foliage. It does well in shallow water, where it will float, or in permanently moist soils where it forms tufts. *Isolepis nodosa* (Knobby Club-rush) has upright green rush-like stems of 0.5–1.5m tall and forms spreading clumps. It is more tolerant of dryness and is excellent for the edges of pools and bog gardens.

Juncus
Rushes

All rushes are excellent for habitat gardening and most prefer moist soils. In fact once a clay-based pool is constructed there is the almost inevitable appearance of rush seedlings. It is recommended that only rushes native to your area be used, for ecological reasons. Some of the most widespread species are *J. pallidus*, *J. procerus*, *J. sarophorus* and *J. subsecundus*.

Lomandra
Mat-rushes

Lomandras are deservedly becoming better known by gardeners. Their adaptability and longevity is wonderful. All the subspecies of *L. confertifolia* are usually less than 0.7m tall. *L. filiformis* (Wattle Mat-rush) forms loose tussocks of greenish-grey foliage and the wattle-like flowers are well displayed during spring and early summer. The closely allied *L. hystrix* and *L. longifolia* provide a bolder impact as they may reach 1m x 1.5–2m.

Orthrosanthus
Morning Flags; Morning Iris

All members of this genus are excellent ornamental plants. Their pale blue to deep blue open-petalled flowers are a marvellous sight during spring and early summer. *O. laxus*, *O. multiflorus* and *O. polystachyus* are the best known species.

Patersonia
Purple Flags

Patersonia occidentalis is the most commonly cultivated species. Its purple or occasionally pale mauve to white, 3-petalled flowers, which are produced on stems longer than the leaves, last one day, only to be

Patersonia occidentalis

replaced in succession over 1–2 months during spring and early summer. Others worth considering are the dwarf species: *P. fragilis*, *P. glabrata* and *P. sericea*.

Poa
Tussock grasses

One needs to be wary of cultivating grasses because many are hardy survivors and thus become better known as weeds. Select only native species which occur in your area. Within the genus *Poa* there are many decorative grasses. *Poa ensiformis* (Purple-sheath Tussock Grass) has bright green leaves and does well in moist, semi-shaded sites. *Poa billardieri* (Common Tussock Grass) can have green or greyish-green to bluish-green leaves and is wonderful for providing a soft accent. *Poa morrisii* (Velvet Tussock Grass) forms a dense upright tussock and its pale purplish flower-spikes are lovely. In moist, shaded sites *P. tenera* (Slender Tussock Grass) can develop into a pleasant groundcover.

Restio tetraphyllus
Tassel-cord Rush

A delightful green rush with brownish tonings which usually grows to 1–2m in height. The arching stems are particularly attractive, especially during flowering and fruiting. The subspecies *trichostachya* is usually smaller and has a denser growth habit. Other restios worth trying include *R. australis* and *R. complanatus*. Dislikes alkalinity.

Stylidium
Trigger Plants

These intriguing plants have a fascinating mechanism controlling the pollination process and seed production. Pollen is deposited and collected through a trigger-like action of the style, activated as insects visit each flower. *S. graminifolium* (Grass Trigger Plant) has pale to deep pink flowers in spikes on stems to 1m tall during spring and summer. It is one of the more readily available species.

Stylidium graminifolium

Stypandra glauca
Nodding Blue-lily

This loose-clumping plant with sprawling to upright stems has its greyish-green leaves arranged in opposite rows. Loose clusters of brilliant blue, starry pendent flowers are produced during spring and early summer. Clumps are rejuvenated by removing old stems.

Thelionema caespitosum
(syn. *Stypandra caespitosa*)
Tufted Blue-lily

The narrow bluish to grey-green leaves combine nicely with the blue or cream starry flowers. The flowers are produced on branched stalks, well above the foliage, during late spring and summer. Butterflies and insects are constant visitors to flowering plants.

Triglochin
Water Ribbons

T. procera needs constant moisture to grow well. Suits wet, low-lying sites and pool edges. The ribbon-like dark green leaves may reach 2m and are usually erect in still water but floating in moving water. A spike of small greenish flowers is displayed above the water. *T. striata* (Streaked Arrow-grass) is a small version of *T. procera*. Insects gather on the foliage above water and below water the foliage is a refuge for many small aquatic creatures.

Vallisneria spiralis
Eel Grass; Ribbon Weed

An aquatic herb with dark green ribbon-like leaves, usually less than 1m. The small white flowers are borne on a spiralling stem in late spring to autumn. As the fruits mature the stems descend to the bottom of the pool.

Villarsia
Marsh Flowers

The dark green glossy spoon-shaped leaves are an attractive feature of marsh flowers. Their yellow 5-petalled flowers are always well-displayed in spring and summer. Villarsias need constant moisture and grow well in muddy sites or in water up to 1m deep. *V. exaltata* and *V. reniformis* adapt very well. Dragonflies, butterflies and other insects visit the flowers.

Groundcovers

Groundcovers give much pleasure with their dense display of foliage and often splendid floral displays. They also serve an important function in promoting plant growth by maintaining a more constant soil temperature. Groundcovers also help to restrict the development of weeds and reduce compaction because heavy rain or water from sprinklers cannot fall directly onto the soil.

Acacia pravissima, prostrate forms
Ovens Wattle

Better known as a tall shrub or small tree — there are now a number of low-growing variants available which are excellent for embankments. 'Golden Carpet' may reach 5m across, while others are less vigorous. All have bright yellow globular flower-heads in spring which contrast well with the greyish-green triangular foliage.

Bauera rubioides
Wiry Bauera

An extremely variable wiry species with all forms having ornamental qualities. The small semi-pendent white to pink flowers peak during spring to early summer. Plants usually grow between 0.2–2m in height. Some of the mounding or semi-clumping forms provide good habitat for small birds.

Brachyscome multifida
Cut-Leaf Daisy

A commonly grown but nonetheless wonderful mounding and spreading daisy which is available with bluish purple, mauve, pink or white flowers. They can bloom through most of the year but are most prolific during spring and summer. Poorly performing plants can be hard-pruned in early spring or mid to late autumn. Butterflies delight in the flowers.

Chrysocephalum apiculatum
(syn. *Helichrysum apiculatum*)
Common Everlasting

Many forms of this attractive species are popular. The yellow to orange-yellow small flower-heads contrast vividly with the greyish-green to grey foliage during spring to autumn. The allied *Chrysocephalum* 'Golden Buttons' is an excellent suckering dwarf everlasting which responds very well to pruning just above ground level during late autumn. *Chrysocephalum semipapposum* (Clustered Everlasting) may take on the form of a dwarf shrub. Plants are like magnets to butterflies.

Chrysocephalum semipapposum

Correa reflexa, dwarf variants
Common Correa

Some of the low-growing coastal selections of this species are highly desirable plants for habitat gardens as their tubular cream or red with green flowers are rich in nectar and bloom for extended periods, often starting in autumn and continuing until spring. The cultivar 'Squat Bell' and selections from south-western Victoria are reliable and attractive.

Crassula helmsii
Swamp Stonecrop

An aquatic herb with bright green foliage. It also does well in boggy soils. Excellent for the edges of pools as it can form a dense cover which helps discourage erosion. May take time to become established if the pool is popular with native ducks and other waterbirds. Small insects often congregate in the foliage near water level.

Einadia nutans
(syn. *Rhagodia nutans*)
Nodding or Climbing Saltbush

A low-spreading shrub with scattered green to grey-green small leaves. The flowers are insignificant but its small succulent red berries in summer and autumn are attractive to birds and lizards. Does well on embankments which are dry for extended periods.

Eremophila
Emu Bushes

Eremophila maculata (Spotted Emu-bush) is extremely variable and is usually seen as a small shrub, but there are low-growing selections available. The red or yellow flowers are produced mainly during winter to spring. Prostrate forms of *E. glabra* as well as *E. serpens* are worth considering too. These species all do best in clay loam soils.

Grevillea curviloba

A bright green, narrow-foliaged shrub with masses of sweetly scented cream flowers during late winter and early spring. The low-growing form can cover large areas but it responds well to pruning. To retain a prostrate growth habit remove any upright stems after flowering. A low form of *G. crithmifolia* and the prostrate *G. synpaheae* also have cream flowers. The former has hairy green leaves while the latter has bronze green hairless leaves. Butterflies and other insects flock to the flowers.

Grevillea juniperina

All of the low-growing variants of this species are worthy of cultivation, especially as their yellow, apricot or red, nectar-rich flowers are produced mainly from winter to summer. Plants may reach 3–4m across if left unpruned. Other prostrate grevilleas which are highly desirable for nectar production include *G.* x *gaudichaudii*, *G. laurifolia* and *G.* 'Poorinda Royal Mantle'.

Grevillea juniperina

Hibbertia
Guinea Flowers

There are a number of low-growing and reliable hibbertias which are captivating when their open-petalled yellow flowers are in full bloom during spring and summer. *H. empetrifolia* is a dense shrub which acts as a climber if it gets half a chance. *H. obtusifolia* has spreading branches and *H. pendunculata* hugs the ground, often self-layering as it goes.

Isotoma fluviatilis ssp. australis
Isotoma

A moisture-loving, self-layering mat plant. Ideal for around the edges of pools or in spots which are moist throughout the year. Its small bright blue flowers are prominent from spring to early winter and may be scattered at other times. The closely allied *Pratia pedunculata* can have white or blue flowers. Plants are rarely without flowers during spring to early winter.

Jasminum suavissimum
Sweet Jasmine

This sweetly fragrant plant can be grown as a groundcover or as an elegant climber. Never prone to being rampant, it is a delightful plant for commonly frequented spots in the garden. The pinkish buds open to white starry blooms over spring and summer. Responds well to pruning.

Kennedia
Coral Peas

Most kennedias are fast-growing but some of the smaller species can be short lived. I think their floral display in spring more than compensates! *K. prostrata* (Running Postman) has brilliant red flowers with a central yellow blotch, while *K. glabrata* (Northcliffe Kennedia) has deep brick-red flowers which are lightly fragrant and are well displayed in racemes on erect stems. *K. rubicunda* (Dusky Coral-pea) and *K. nigricans* (Black Coral-pea) are extremely vigorous and require a large area for their development.

Leucophyta brownii
(syn. *Calocephalus brownii*)
Cushion Bush

An outstanding silvery-foliaged mounding plant which copes with coastal extremes and also does well inland in open sunny sites. The globular cream flower-heads are displayed over summer months and insects such as butterflies are attracted to them. Pruning helps promote bushy growth.

Marsilea
Nardoo

Nardoos are terrestrial or aquatic ferns which do well on the edges of pools, in shallow water or in depressions which are intermittently wet. The leaves, like those of a four-leaf-clover, are very decorative. *M. drummondii* (Common Nardoo), *M. hirsuta* (Short-fruit Nardoo), *M. mutica* (Banded Nardoo) and *M. costulifera* are popular. Their dense coverage can provide refuge for small aquatic fauna. In temperate regions the creeping rhizomes may die back and the plant may become dormant.

Mentha
Native Mints

The aromatic foliage of culinary mints is well known and the Australian species are true to type. *Mentha australis*, *M. diemenica*, *M. laxiflora* and *M. satureoides* are easy to grow. They can also have the same overtaking ways as their exotic relatives. They are ideal for the edges of pools and in shady moist sites with ferns. The small white, mauve or pinkish flowers attract insects when they bloom over spring to autumn.

Morinda jasminoides
Sweet Morinda

The sweetly scented, starry white to orange flowers are clustered in well displayed heads over late spring and summer, followed by decorative orange to red fleshy fruits. Likes organic-rich soils. In shady sites it climbs but in semi-open or open sites it develops as a groundcover. May need to prune young erect stems.

Myoporum parvifolium
Creeping Boobialla; Creeping Myoporum

A variable species with bright green to purplish-green fleshy, narrow leaves. The white or rarely pink flowers can be produced in profusion over spring to early autumn, followed by small whitish berries. Excellent for heavy soils, especially on embankments as it is self-layering.

Myoporum parvifolium

Myriophyllum
Water Milfoils

These aquatic or semi-aquatic plants are excellent for growing in shallow water or beside pools where they stabilise the edges. Their finely foliaged stems have a soft, lacy appearance. Plants provide a habitat for small animals such as fish and frogs and for many insects. *Myriophyllum caput-medusae* (Cat-tail), *M. variifolium* (Variable Water-milfoil) and *M. papillosum* are recommended species. All water-milfoils have the capacity to cover large areas.

Nymphoides crenata

Nymphoides
Marshworts

Most of these charming aquatic plants have glossy, rounded leaves which float on water. The yellow or cream to white, fringed flowers are well-displayed above the foliage during late spring to early autumn. *Nymphoides crenata* (Wavy Marshwort), *N. geminata* (Star Fringe) and *N. indica* (Water Snowflake) are among the most popular.

Ottelia ovalifolia
Swamp Lily

An excellent pool plant with floating elliptical dark green leaves. The flowers are up to 7.5cm across and white with a deep reddish purple central blotch. They are produced during late spring to early autumn.

Pimelea humilis
Common or Small Rice-flower

A low-growing, suckering plant with crowded, small greyish-green leaves on erect to spreading stems. The creamy-white flower-heads are well-displayed on ends of the stems during spring and summer. Butterflies adore the flowers.

Pratia pedunculata

See *Isotoma fluviatilis*, page 42

Pultenaea pedunculata
Matted Bush-pea

This self-layering pea-plant can form lovely fine-foliaged mats of 1–2m across. In spring the yellow and red, yellow, lemon yellow, orange or pale pink flowers can envelop the foliage to create an enchanting display which is also enjoyed by butterflies and insects.

Scaevola
Fan-flowers

A number of fan-flowers are excellent groundcovering plants, as they can flower for most of the year and have a glorious peak flowering over spring and summer. Butterflies and other insects delight in their nectar supply. *Scaevola aemula* with its many selections is captivating. *S. striata* can have pink, mauve or purplish blue flowers. The small-flowered *S. pallida* and *S. albida* are just as handsome with their white, pinkish or mauve-blue flowers.

Scaevola aemula 'Purple Fanfare'

Spyridium parvifolium 'Austraflora Nimbus'
Australian Dusty Miller

This prostrate variant makes an appealing groundcover, especially in semi-shaded sites. Its flowers are insignificant but the surrounding floral leaves are grey and contrast with the deep green leaves elsewhere.

Viola hederacea
Australian Violet

A lover of moist-sheltered sites, this charming ever-flowering violet has white and violet-blue flowers. 'Baby Blue' has bluish violet flowers while 'White Glory' has lightly fragrant white flowers. Plants may cover 1–2m across.

Xanthosia rotundifolia
Southern Cross

A mounding low shrub with toothed, rounded green leaves. The wonderful cross-like clusters of white to cream flowers, which often age to pink or burgundy, are produced mainly during spring and summer at the ends of elongated stalks. Insects love the flowers.

Climbers

Climbers are utilised in many ways. Commonly they are used as a screen or to clothe areas with foliage. At other times they are grown purely for ornamental purposes. Some people like to grow them on a structure, while other gardeners would rather have them wander over, through and around nearby plants. The vigour of some climbers is often misunderstood by experienced and inexperienced gardeners!

Billardiera
Apple-berries

Billardieras are long-flowering, mainly over late spring through to early autumn. Generally they are light-foliaged climbers with flared tubular flowers. Well-established shrubs or trees can easily accommodate a climbing billardiera. *B. bicolor* (Painted Billardiera) has white to cream flowers with violet stripes. *B. cymosa* (Sweet Apple Berry) produces greenish-white, pinkish or blue flowers. *B. longiflora* (Purple Apple Berry) has greenish-yellow flowers that are followed by fleshy elongated purplish berries. *B. ringens* (Chapman River Climber) has flowers which seemingly magically change from orange-yellow to brilliant red as they mature, and *B. scandens* (Common Apple Berry) has pale greenish-yellow flowers.

Cissus antarctica
Watervine

A vigorous and very effective member of the grape family which has lustrous, broad, toothed leaves. In summer the small cream flowers are followed by small black, globular berries which are food for birds. Can be grown in containers but usually needs regular pruning.

Clematis

The starry white or cream flowers of male and female clematis plants are exquisite during spring to early summer. One of the delights of a female clematis is being able to view the fluffy seed-heads with back lighting in autumn. These seeds are a food source for birds and some are used for nest construction. *C. aristata* (Goat's Beard) and the closely allied *C. glycinoides* and *C. pubescens* prefer a moist, semi-shaded site for their roots, but they love to climb over the foliage of other plants or structures. *C. microphylla* (Small-leaved Clematis) is more tolerant. Butterflies and other insects are attracted to the flowers.

Hardenbergia

Hardenbergias are appreciated for their quick growth and floriferous displays. The Native Lilac or Wild Sarsaparilla, *Hardenbergia comptoniana* has broad, dark green foliage and lightly scented, blue-purple-peas, creating a superb display during late winter and spring. Purple Coral Pea, or False Sarsaparilla, *H. violacea* is an excellent climber or scrambler for heavy, rocky soils. The purple flowers are profuse during winter and spring. The extremely vigorous but not fully frost-tolerant cultivar 'Happy Wanderer' has mauve-purple flowers while 'Free 'n Easy' has white flowers.

Hibbertia
Guinea Flowers

Although most hibbertias are shrubs, there are a couple of climbers which are valuable for attracting insects. *H. scandens* (Climbing Guinea-flower) is very vigorous with strong twining stems. Its large yellow flowers peak in spring and summer. Best not planted in close proximity to doors, windows and outdoor seating areas because of its strong floral perfume. Enjoy it at a distance! *H. dentata* (Trailing Guinea-flower) is more dainty. The yellow flowers are smaller and it has lovely bronze to reddish young growth. It may regenerate prolifically in some regions, so it is best not to grow it near bushland.

Jasminum suavissimum, see page 42. *Morinda jasminoides*, see page 43.

Parsonsia brownii
Twining Silkpod

This vigorous climber has long, dark green leaves which have a yellowish undersurface. The small, hairy, yellow-green starry flowers are borne in loose clusters in the upper axils during spring and summer. They are followed by cylindrical seed pods of about 8cm long which open on ripening, revealing seed attached to silky plumes. Common Silkpod or Monkey Rope, *P. straminea*, has leaves with a greyish undersurface and fruits to 25cm long.

Passiflora aurantia
Blunt-leaved Passionfruit

A lovely climber with dark green, usually three-lobed leaves. It produces marvellous flowers over spring and summer which open white and mature to pinkish-red. This is a food plant for the larvae of the Glasswing Butterfly. The allied *P. cinnabarina* (Crimson Passionflower) has wrinkled leaves and conspicuous coppery-red flowers during spring and early summer. Both of these can cover large areas.

Passiflora aurantia

Ferns and fern allies

Ferns are excellent for providing different foliage textures and forms. Although many do not have specific wildlife-attracting attributes they are very useful for planting in moist or wet sites where wildlife tend to visit and congregate. This is often the case during extended hot periods.

Blechnum
Water Ferns

These ferns are moisture-lovers, as the common name implies. The larger species *B. minus* (Soft Water Fern), *B. nudum* (Fishbone Water Fern) and *B. wattsii* (Hard Water Fern) are adaptable and can grow fronds to about 1m long.

Cyathea australis
See Tree Ferns.

Doodia
Rasp Ferns

Some ferns provide more than just attractive green foliage. The low-growing *Doodia media* (Common Rasp Fern) is an example, with its alluring purplish-pink new growth over late spring and summer. *D. caudata* (Small Rasp Fern) and *D. aspera* (Prickly Rasp Fern) are ornamental too. All of these ferns tolerate sunshine as long as their root system is kept moist.

Gleichenia
Coral Ferns

Gleichenia microphylla (Scrambling Coral Fern) and *G. dicarpa* (Pouched Coral Fern) are closely allied. Initially both may be slow to develop but they can form thickets of branched fern fronds after many years, to 1m or more in height, providing refuge for small animals and birds. They are lovely plants for the edges of pools or in permanently moist areas among other plants, such as melaleucas and leptospermums. The closely related Fan Fern genus, with *Sticherus lobatus* and *S. tener* also like similar conditions.

Todea barbara
King Fern

An outstanding fern which develops a short, broad trunk from which a number of crowns of dark green, shiny fronds to 2.5m long emanate. It requires soils which are constantly moist.

Tree Ferns

Australia has several popular native tree ferns. Cyatheas are among the most commonly grown tree ferns. *Cyathea australis* (Hard Tree Fern) is very adaptable and tolerates slightly dry sites well. *C. cooperi* (Scaly Tree Fern) has ravishing new fronds and is quick growing. *Dicksonia antarctica* (Soft Tree Fern) must have moist soil to do well and it prefers a protected site. These three tree ferns are readily available and are usually priced at so much per metre of trunk. Young sporelings may lack the dramatic effect gained from tall imposing trunks but they develop lengthy fronds fairly quickly to produce a handsome effect.

Palms

Some palms provide habitat for nesting sites and some can be prolific producers of fruits. Birds such as the White-bearded and Torresian Imperial Pigeon feast on palm fruits. The flowers are often an outstanding source of nectar for insects.

Archontophoenix cunninghamiana
Bangalow Palm

A tall slender-trunked palm which needs constant moisture. Its glorious crown of fronds has made it very popular. The large panicles of pink to lilac flowers appear during summer to early autumn and are followed by waxy, bright red, globular fruit. They are usually slow-growing in temperate regions and dislike frost while they are young.

Carpentaria acuminata
Carpentaria Palm

An elegant palm with dark green fronds; recommended for growing only in tropical regions as it is very susceptible to damage from low temperatures. The prominent large panicles of white flowers are produced during the latter part of the year and are followed by the decorative, smooth, bright red fruit which are devoured by birds such as the Torresian Imperial Pigeon.

Linospadix monostachya
Walking Stick Palm

A short, very slender-stemmed palm which does well in tropical, subtropical and temperate areas and develops best in full shade in organic-rich soils which are moist throughout the year. During late winter to summer the small greenish flowers appear on a slender pendent stem and give way to the small, waxy, yellow-orange to red fruits.

Shrubs

Small, medium and large shrubs are usually the major component of most gardens, providing endless scope for variation in choice of foliage, form and flower. All of the shrubs described in this section help to create a wildlife habitat. Some of them have the capacity to develop into small trees if the cultivation conditions are well suited to their needs.

Acacia
Wattles

With over 700 different acacias to choose from it is difficult to restrict this selection to just a few. Butterflies are strongly attracted to the nectar and the seed is a major food source for birds such as pigeons and parrots. *Acacia calamifolia* (Wallowa) is a rounded, small shrub with narrow foliage. A hot sunny site is best. Bower or River Wattle, *A. cognata* is a lovely tall shrub or small tree with aromatic, pendulous, narrow foliage and pale yellow balls in late winter or spring. The closely allied *A. leprosa* (Cinnamon Wattle) is usually not as tall and the flowers are lemon-yellow. *A. drummondii* has many variants with small ferny leaves and rod-like flower-heads during winter to spring — a stunning sight! *A. myrtifolia* (Myrtle Wattle) is very quick-growing and is best regarded as a short-term shrub. The cream to yellow balls in late winter and early spring are followed by copious seed pods. *A. retinodes* (Wirilda) can bloom for most of the year but it peaks in late spring and summer. Two extremely prickly, shrubby wattles, *A. paradoxa* (Hedge Wattle) and *A. verticillata* (Prickly Moses) are excellent refuge plants for small birds. For other Wattles, see Trees, page 55.

Acacia drummondii

Plants for pool surrounds

Code for plant groups

f = fern
tu = tussock or clump-forming plants
g = groundcover
ss = small shrub
ts = tall shrub
t = tree

Acacia cognata	ts-t
A. leprosa	ts
Allocasuarina torulosa	t
A. littoralis	t
Alocasia macrorhizos	tu
Bauera rubioides	g-ss
Callistemon salignus	ts
Chionochloa pallida	tu
Coprosma quadrifida	ss
Cordyline petiolaris	ss-ts
C. stricta	ss-ts
Cyathea australis	f
Dianella tasmanica	tu
Doodia aspera	f
D. caudata	f
Gahnia sieberiana	tu
Goodia lotifolia	ts
Grevillea acanthifolia	ss
Hibbertia empetrifolia	g-ss
Kunzea ericoides	ts
Leptospermum petersonii	ts
L. polygalifolium	ts
Melaleuca ericifolia	t
M. quinquenervia	t
M. rhaphiophylla	t
M. squamea	ts
Mentha laxiflora	g
Patersonia occidentalis	tu
Poa ensiformis	tu
P. labillardieri	tu
Thelionema caespitosa	tu
Viminaria juncea	ts
Viola hederacea	g

Alectryon subcinereus
Bird's Eye; Native Quince; Smooth Rambutan

A bushy, tall shrub with multiple trunks. The ferny leaves have 4–6 leathery, glossy, green leaflets. Flowers are small but the seeds are very decorative. *A. coriaceus* may develop into a small tree. It prefers a semi-shaded site while young. Seeds from both of these species are eagerly devoured by birds.

Austromyrtus dulcis
Midgen Berry

The pinkish-bronze, young growth of this small, low, spreading shrub is appealing. The mature leaves are dark green and the small white, open-petalled flowers bloom mainly during summer and autumn. The brownish-white to mauve globular fruits are edible.

Baeckea

Baeckea has many ornamental members and some of the shrubby ones are notable insect-attractants over the summer months. *Baeckea astarteoides* is a small shrub with clustered small leaves. It produces its dainty pink flowers over late spring to early autumn. *B. linifolia* (Weeping Baeckea) is a handsome medium-sized shrub with graceful weeping branches. The small white flowers are borne in the upper axils over summer and autumn. *B. virgata* (Twiggy Baeckea) can grow tall and is excellent for screening; there are also some dwarf selections available.
B. behri (Broom Baeckea) does best in warm temperate regions where its lovely clear white or pale pink flowers are a delight during late spring and summer.

Banksia

Banksias are extremely important plants for wildlife because their nectar is a food source for many birds, animals and insects.

Except for some of the shrubby Western Australian species, most banksias are adaptable to cultivation. Those worth trying include *B. blechnifolia*, *B. petiolaris* and *B. repens*, plus the low-spreading forms of some species which are usually more upright, such as *B. integrifolia*, *B. marginata*, *B. serrata* and *B. spinulosa*.

The shrubby *B. canei* (Mountain Banksia) tolerates very low temperatures. *B. ericifolia* (Heath Banksia) is very popular with its large erect candles of orange, orange-red, cream and red, or burgundy flowers over autumn to spring. This banksia may reach the size of a small tree. Another species which can grow quite tall is *B. marginata* (Silver Banksia) but there are also shrubby selections available. Its pale to bright yellow flower-spikes are produced during spring to autumn. *B. spinulosa* (Hill Banksia) which flowers during the same period, is wonderfully variable. Taller selections make effective screening plants. The flushes of new growth are a decorative hallmark of some banksias. *B. oblongifolia* (Fern-leaved Banksia) has lovely rusty-brown new shoots. Its sizeable flower-heads are pale yellow and produced over autumn and winter.

Breynia

These two small- to medium-sized shrubs are best grown in subtropical and tropical regions. They lack strong floral attributes but their bright red or orange berries are ornamental and birds feast upon them. *Breynia oblongifolia* (Coffee Bush) has arching branches and responds well to pruning. It can be kept small.
B. cernua has a graceful habit and may need supplementary watering.

Buckinghamia celsissima
Ivory Curl

Often a slow-growing small tree, but it can be kept as a shrub by pruning. Flushes of new growth are pink to red. The margins of leaves can be smooth or lobed and the sprays of creamy-white, sweetly scented flowers can be outstanding during summer and autumn. Plants can take a number of years to flower but when they do there will be a hive of wildlife activity.

Buckinghamia celsissima

Bursaria spinosa
Sweet Bursaria

A highly desirable plant for wildlife habitat. The prickly foliage makes it valuable as a refuge plant. During late spring to early autumn, the sweetly scented, small cream flowers are regularly attended by butterflies. It is a host plant for the larvae of a number of butterflies, including the rare Eltham Copper Butterfly. Sometimes it will develop into a small tree. Responds very well to pruning or coppicing.

Callicarpa pedunculata
Velvet Leaf

A small to tall shrub with soft, velvety leaves and small lilac to purple flowers in loose clusters on older wood during spring. The bright purple fruits are eaten by birds. Does best in northern Australia but also succeeds in temperate regions if given a protected spot.

Callistemon
Bottlebrushes

You will never be short of nectar-feeding birds if you have a few bottlebrushes in your garden. Their bold floral displays in spring and summer are stunning. Have you tried planting two or three different coloured bottlebrushes in the same hole? The tall shrubs are very useful for screening purposes. C. 'Harkness', C. 'Kings Park Special', C. citrinus 'Splendens' and C. viminalis with its many selections, all have red flowers. C. 'Mauve Mist', C. 'Perth Pink' and C. pallidus with its lemon yellow flowers offer colour variety. C. comboynensis has red brushes and there are low-growing selections as well as taller ones; it can flower most of the year.

An extra flush of flowers in autumn can be encouraged by fertilising in autumn and spring.

Caper White Butterfly resting on *Callistemon* 'Mauve Mist'

Calothamnus
Net-bushes; Claw Flowers

Closely allied to *Callistemon*, plants of this genus are excellent for attracting nectar-feeding birds. *Calothamnus quadrifidus* (Common Net-bush) is a variable species of 2–4 m x 2–5 m which has pine-like green to grey leaves. Brilliant red, claw-like flowers are arranged on one side of the branches or sometimes in a bottlebrush fashion during late spring to late summer. Other Calothamnus worth trying are C. homalophyllus, C. validus, C. villosus (all of which have red flowers) and C. rupestris which has pinkish to pale red flowers.

Calytrix
Fringe Myrtles

The brightest of white, starry flowers combined with pale pink buds amidst short teeth-like leaves during spring make *Calytrix alpestris* (Snow Myrtle) a highly desirable small shrub. It appreciates supplementary watering during extended dry periods and pruning after flowering promotes compactness. The allied C. tetragona (Fringe Myrtle) white to deep pink flowers over the same period, while C. glutinosa will display its charming lilac to light purple flowers during late spring and early summer. Excellent butterfly attractors.

Cassia
Cassias

Nearly all members of this genus attract wildlife. The scented flowers are regularly visited by butterflies such as the Australian Painted Lady, Common Brown, Grass Yellow and Icilius Blue and larvae of the latter two use them as food plants. The seeds are often eaten by birds. The small shrub C. artemisioides (Silver Cassia) produces lovely yellow flowers for most of the year, with a peak in spring. The flowers contrast with the greyish-green to silvery-ferny foliage. C. brewsteri (Leichhardt Bean) is taller and may reach small tree proportions doing best in subtropical and tropical regions. This cassia has pendent sprays of dark cream and pink flowers — spectacular against the dark green pinnate leaves during autumn. It may also flower at other times.

Chamelaucium
Waxflowers

Chamelaucium uncinatum (Geraldton Wax) is well known, with its tea-tree-like flowers in many hues of pink and purple as well as cream and white. Flowering is mainly during late winter and spring. Although often marketed as a small shrub it can develop to over 5m in height, but it does respond very well to pruning! The smaller C. ciliatum is available as greyish- or green-foliaged selections. In spring to early summer the flower-buds are pink, opening to small white flowers which age to pink or pinkish red.

Chamelaucium uncinatum

Chorizema
Flame Peas

The outstanding brilliance of chorizemas in flower has made them popular. Among the more reliable are C. ilicifolium (Holly Flame Pea), C. cordatum and C. varium; all produce their flowers of orange, red, yellow and pink during late winter to early summer. Plants may climb if they are able to gain support from other shrubs. Butterflies visit the flowers.

After hibernation, cold-blooded reptiles love to bask in the sun — as this Blotched Blue-tongue is doing on its front porch.

Crimson rosellas are voracious consumers of plant seeds. They can also be excellent for controlling gall insects in eucalypt leaves. (PHOTO: BILL KING)

A colourful St Andrew's Cross spider is waiting for dinner to arrive. Spider webs look magical in the morning when they are adorned with droplets of dew.

Native bees and other insects in search of nectar find the Poached-egg Daisy, *Polycalymna stuartii* (*Myriocephalus stuartii*) most attractive. This daisy is best suited to warm, temperate or semi-arid regions.

Cordyline
Palm Lilies

Often we seek plants for narrow sites. The suckering cordylines which have erect, woody stems, of 2–5m tall, topped with strap-like leaves can be the perfect answer. *Cordyline stricta* (Slender Palm Lily) tolerates plenty of sunshine. The pale purple to violet, starry flowers are in prominent sprays near the ends of the stem during spring and summer. They are followed by small, globular, black or purplish berries. *C. petiolaris* is similar but has broader, larger leaves and red berries. *C. congesta*, similar to *C. stricta*, has orange-red berries. *C. rubra* has broad leaves, lilac flowers and glossy scarlet berries.

Correa

Correas are renowned for their nectar production and their ability to cope with adverse conditions, such as shady, dry sites or exposure to salt-laden winds.

Correa backhousiana is a bushy shrub with dark green leaves and rusty-coloured new growth. The cream to pale green bells are produced over winter and spring. *C. lawrenciana* (Mountain Correa) is variable and different varieties are available. The buff to reddish, narrow flowers tend to be hidden by the foliage, but honeyeaters are in no way deterred. Occasionally *C. lawrenciana* grows to the size of a small tree but plants respond well to pruning. The bright red bells of *C.* 'Mannii' are seen mainly during autumn and spring but plants may also have some flowers at other times.

Dodonaea
Hop Bushes

Hop bushes are excellent for tolerating extended dry periods. Their display of winged fruits is often eye-catching. The tall, shrubby *Dodonaea sinuolata* ssp. *acrodentata*, often sold under the wrong name of *D. adenophora*, does best in a warm

Dodonaea sinuolata

sunny site. It has ferny leaves and plentiful reddish 'hops' during the latter half of the year. *D. triquetra* (Large-leaf Hop Bush), also a tall shrub, is very quick-growing and produces 'hops' which are brown to purplish with yellow tonings. Pigeons are avid feeders on hop bush seed.

Epacris
Heaths

The two most commonly grown members of this genus are marvellous plants. *Epacris impressa* (Common Heath) is an upright small to medium shrub with short, prickly leaves and white, pink or red tubular flowers which bloom in winter and spring. *E. longiflora* (Fuchsia Heath) has pendent, tubular flowers of red, tipped with white. They are often produced on long, spreading branches and provide a dramatic effect during winter to summer. These plants are a nectar-feeding bird's delight. They respond very well to medium or hard pruning.

Eremophila
Emu Bushes

Groundcovering forms of *E. glabra* and *E. maculata* are described on page 41. The taller forms are also recommended, especially for areas of moderate or low rainfall.

Eriostemon myoporoides
Long-leaved Waxflower

A very reliable and showy shrub with aromatic, greyish-green leaves. The pale pink buds open to white starry flowers and are profuse during winter and spring. Excellent for attracting small insects.

Eugenia reinwardtiana
Beach Cherry

This slow-growing, decorative, small to tall bushy shrub has dark green, thick leaves. Fluffy, white flowers are produced usually sporadically during winter to summer. The red, juicy, more or less globular, edible berries are about 2cm across and are seen on plants from spring to autumn.

Eupomatia laurina
Bolwarra; Copper Laurel

This plant has attractive foliage and can reach small tree proportions but it is usually a tall shrub and is readily controlled by pruning. The thick, glossy leaves often have coppery or bronze tonings. Highly fragrant cream or white flowers are seen in late spring to early summer, followed by semi-globular fruits which are edible. Tolerates light frosts.

Goodenia ovata
Hop Goodenia

A quick-growing, shrubby species with bright to dark green leaves and bright yellow flowers which are produced over late spring and summer and are excellent for attracting butterflies and other insects. Plants may become a bit straggly but they respond well to hard pruning. There is also a prostrate selection available. Both are ideal for planting beneath a shading canopy. The suckering and matting *G. humilis* is highly desirable for the edges of pools or in wet, sunny sites.

Goodia lotifolia
Golden Tip; Clover Tree

A fast-growing, tall shrub which copes well with low light. The bluish-green to greyish-green foliage contrasts with the lightly fragrant creamy-yellow pea flowers, seen during winter and spring. Responds well to pruning and can be very useful for screening purposes in semi-shaded sites but it may become open in heavy shade.

Grevillea
Grevilleas

A popular genus that provides some of the best nectar-producing plants. Grevillea flowers attract nectar-feeding birds, many insects including beautiful and often exquisite butterflies, plus insect-eating birds. A limited selection is described here. Referral to the Further Reading references will give plenty of other options for suitable grevilleas.

Grevillea acanthifolia is a spreading, prickly-foliaged low shrub which produces pinkish-purple toothbrush-like flower-heads, mainly during spring and summer. It is good for wet soils and insects are attracted to the flowers. *G. aquifolium* (Prickly Grevillea) is extremely variable — it can be anything from a low groundcover to a tall shrub. All selections have attributes which make them valuable for cultivation. Nectar-feeding birds are regular visitors to the red and green toothbrush flowers which bloom mainly during spring and early summer. *G. australis* (Alpine Grevillea) advertises itself during spring and summer with a strong, sometimes overpowering, floral perfume emanating from the small, cream flowers that are attended by many insects.

G. banksii (Red Silky Oak) is one of the parents of many of the showy hybrid grevilleas which have become fairly commonplace in recent years, such as *G.* 'Robyn Gordon', *G.* 'Pink Surprise', *G.* 'Misty Pink', *G.* 'Ned Kelly', *G.* 'Honey Gem' and *G.* 'Superb', all of which are excellent for attracting birds and insects. The tall, shrubby form of *G. banksii*,

Grevillea intricata

sometimes sold as 'Forsters Form' is an excellent plant for frost-free regions and can produce the lovely red brushes over most of spring and early summer with sporadic bursts at other times.

G. intricata has reddish stems and much-divided leaves with very narrow segments. The sweetly scented, cream flowers are arranged in tapering sprays near the ends of the branches during spring. It is a superlative refuge plant for small birds. For dense, entangled foliage it is hard to surpass.

The tall, bushy form of *G. rosmarinifolia* (Rosemary Grevillea) is often grown as a hedge. There are dwarf and small, shrubby selections and hybrids, which are good value and produce plenty of pink to red with cream flowers during winter and spring. Those worth considering include 'Lara Dwarf', 'Nana' and 'Scarlet Sprite'.

G. shiressii (Blue Grevillea) seems an unlikely bird-attracting plant at a distance because it seems to lack flowers, but on close inspection during spring and summer the greenish-blue and purplish-brown translucent flowers will be found among the sizeable dark green leaves. A strong-growing tall shrub, responds well to pruning and clipping. One of the best bird-attracting grevilleas.

Hakea

Hakeas are closely allied to grevilleas and have similar bird- and insect-attracting attributes. *H. laurina* (Pincushion Hakea) is a popular, tall shrub but it can become unstable if watered and fertilised. The glorious red and cream flower-balls are produced over autumn and winter. The closely allied *H. petiolaris* (Sea Urchin Hakea) has broad, greyish leaves and cream with maroon flower-heads. *H. orthorrhyncha* (Bird Hakea) is another tall shrub but it has needle-like leaves and brilliant red flowers in clusters along the old wood during winter and early spring — a breathtaking sight when backlit.

H. sericea (Silky Hakea) and its allies are excellent nesting and refuge plants because of their prickly nature. During winter and early spring plants can produce a profuse display of white or pale pink flowers. The prickly *H. lissocarpha* (Honeybush) is variable in size and foliage with sweetly scented, white to pink flowers which can virtually envelop the foliage during winter. *H. verrucosa* is marvellous as it can start flowering in early autumn and continue until early spring. The flowers are initially cream to pale pink but mature to deep pink or reddish. *H. clavata* (Coastal Hakea) is a low shrub which has the appearance of a succulent, with its thick fleshy leaves, however, there's a prickly surprise lurking in their pointed tips. In late winter and early spring the deep pink buds open to paler hues and emit a strong fragrance.

An excellent plant for waterlogged soils, *H. nodosa* (Yellow Hakea), bears cream to yellow, heavily scented flowers among its narrow green to bluish-green leaves in autumn and winter.

Hakea lissocarpha

Hymenanthera dentata
Tree violet

A spiny-branched, tall shrub with small, dark green leaves. The small, tubular, strongly fragrant, pale yellow flowers bloom in late winter and spring and are arranged in clusters on the branches. Excellent for insect attraction and as a refuge plant. Recommended for dry, rocky sites.

Hypocalymma
Myrtles

Plants which produce flowers that change colour as they mature are captivating. *Hypocalymma angustifolium* (White Myrtle) should to my mind be called the Coconut-ice Plant, as this fine-foliaged, small shrub has flowers during winter and spring which open as white but then gain deeper shades of pink, providing a lovely mixed effect. The broad-leaved *H. cordifolium* has bright green, spreading leaves and reddish new stems, which help to set off the small white flowers very effectively.

Jacksonia scoparia
Dogwood

This lovely, tall shrub belongs to a sadly neglected genus which has many choice plants. Its narrow, greyish-green foliage has the same quality as she-oak foliage, and the exquisitely fragrant, small, yellow to orange pea-flowers are profuse during spring.

Kunzea

Kunzea pulchella provides periods of superb combinations of floral and foliage brilliance during spring and summer. The magnificent heads of scarlet to bright red flowers contrast with the silky-hairy, greyish-green leaves and are a honeyeater's delight. *K. baxteri* (Crimson Kunzea) is another exciting tall shrub. It may

Kunzea baxteri

take a number of years to flower but, when it does, winter and spring will be colourful. *K. ericoides* (Burgan) produces its masses of white to pale cream flowers over summer. Insects find them alluring just as they do with the scented flowers of the Tick Bush or White Kunzea, *K. ambigua* during mid-spring to early summer.

Leptospermum
Tea-trees

Most tea-trees are very adaptable to a wide range of conditions. They are reliable plants for cultivation and many are extremely floriferous. Small- to medium-sized shrubs include: *Leptospermum squarrosum* (Peach or Blossom Tea-tree) with its white to pale to deep pink flowers borne in autumn on older wood; *L. rotundifolium* (Round-leaf Tea-tree) available in many forms, with large, well displayed, white, pink, bluish pink or mauve flowers in spring; and *L. macrocarpum* is well worth considering. It can have greenish-white, cream, pink or reddish petals and the coppery to bronze new foliage is superb. Tea-trees are mainly popular with butterflies and insects but *L. macrocarpum* is visited by nectar-feeding birds.

Leptospermum polygalifolium

If you prefer a tall shrub, your options are wide open. *L. lanigerum* (Woolly Tea-tree) has white flowers during spring and early summer and some variants have lovely greyish foliage. (There is a handsome selection of moderate proportions known as *L. lanigerum* 'Pendulous'.) *L. petersonii* (Lemon-scented Tea-tree) has foliage with a superb fragrance. During summer the white to pale cream flowers provide plenty of nectar for butterflies and other insects. The bronze to reddish new growth is a bonus. *L. polygalifolium* has variants occurring throughout its extensive range from north-eastern Qld to south-eastern NSW. In late spring and summer the production of white to cream flowers is prolific.

Lomatia

A member of the Protea family which could be better known as there are many highly desirable lomatias, with the majority flowering during summer and early autumn. *Lomatia silaifolia* (Wild Parsley Bush) does not usually get taller than 2m. Sometimes it may be a dwarf compact plant. Its ferny, deep green leaves contrast nicely with the elongated, terminal, fragrant flower-heads. *L. fraseri* (Silky Lomatia) is taller. The leaves usually have rusty hairs on the undersurface and its sweetly-scented flowers are produced from the leaf axils.

Melaleuca
Honey-myrtles; Paperbarks

Melaleuca is closely allied to *Callistemon*, and both are very important for attracting wildlife to gardens. Most species are also proven plants for a wide range of soil and climatic conditions.

An uncommon plant in gardens, *Melaleuca calothamnoides* has brick red brushes, which are partly hidden by the green to bluish-green narrow leaves. They are produced during autumn to spring with a peak in the later months. A honeyeater's delight! Totem Poles or Cross-leaved Honey-myrtle, *M. decussata* is a small to tall shrub. It doesn't attract honeyeaters but insects attend the small pink or purplish brushes which are produced on the older wood during spring and summer. Both *M. decussata* and *M. squamea* (Swamp Honey-myrtle) are excellent for wet soils, with the latter, an upright plant useful for narrow places, producing mauve to pinkish, globular flower-heads during spring. *M. filifolia* (Wiry Honey-myrtle) prefers a sunny dry site and in late spring and early summer its large mauve-pink to pink pom-poms can be outstanding. Butterflies agree!

Other insect-attracting melaleucas include *M. ericifolia* (Swamp Paperbark), a tall shrub or ultimately a small tree with lovely pale papery bark. In spring, the canopy can be covered with small, cream, sweetly-scented brushes. A wonderful plant for growing in copses as it can sucker once plants are well established. *M. nodosa*, *M. viminea*, *M. squarrosa* and *M. elliptica* are all good food plants.

Microcitrus australasica
Finger Lime

This small to tall shrub is a member of the citrus family and is best suited to tropical and subtropical regions. It is an interesting plant with thorny branches and small but broad, dark green, glossy leaves. Sweetly-scented white flowers in late summer and autumn are followed by cylindrical, green to reddish purple fruits with luscious edible flesh. Butterflies are common visitors to flowering plants.

Mirbelia oxyloboides
Mountain Mirbelia

A floriferous, small shrub with small, olive-green leaves. The yellow with orange, lightly fragrant pea-flowers which bloom during spring are usually surrounded by butterflies engaged in feverish activity, gathering nectar. Suitable for hedging.

Myoporum
Boobiallas

Flowering myoporums are favoured by butterflies. *M. floribundum* (Slender Myoporum) is a graceful, small to medium shrub with horizontal to ascending branches and pendent, narrow, green leaves. The strongly scented, starry white flowers are prominently displayed during spring and summer on the upper side of the branches.

Olearia
Daisy-bushes

The reputation of perennial and semi-woody daisies for profuse and captivating flowering displays is legion. *Olearia* is an outstanding woody species. Butterflies like them too!

Olearia phlogopappa (Dusty Daisy-bush) is available as selections with different flower colours, giving us the choice of white, pale pink, deep pink, mauve, purple or blue during the spring months. Generally plants rarely get taller than 2.5m. A regular yearly light pruning helps promote bushy growth. *O. tomentosa* can grow to a similar height and the sizeable white or blue daisies are produced mainly in spring and early summer, but they may also appear at other times. It has broad, toothed leaves which are dull green above with grey hairs on the undersurface. Virtually any *Olearia* is valuable for attracting butterflies.

Olearia tormentosa

Phebalium
Phebaliums; Satinwoods

These are members of the citrus family and closely allied to *Crowea* and *Eriostemon*. The small-growing *P. lamprophyllum* (Shiny Phebalium) is one of the most adaptable plants around. It copes with a hot, dry, open site and is just as comfortable in a shady, dry or moist spot. Its clusters of white to cream starry flowers are profuse in late winter and spring.

P. squameum ssp. *squameum* (Satinwood) grows much taller and is excellent for screening. In spring, the loose clusters of white flowers are shown off to advantage against the glossy, dark green leaves.

Pimelea
Rice Flowers

Pimelea flowers are undoubtedly among the favourites of butterflies as food plants. *Pimelea ferruginea* (Coastal Rice-flower), a low shrub, is available in many forms, all with flowers of differing shades of pink, blooming during late winter and spring, with the semi-globular heads well displayed above the compact, glossy, green foliage. Regular light pruning after flowering is beneficial. *P. imbricata* is a low mounding plant and its bright lolly pink or pale pink flower-heads are a delight during late spring and early summer. Further flowering can be encouraged by pruning hard in late December.

Pittosporum

Pittosporum phylliraeoides (Weeping Pittosporum) may grow up to be a small tree but it is normally slow-growing. The usually pendent branchlets are adorned with sweetly-scented, cream to yellow flowers during spring and summer and are followed by small orange berries. *P. rhombifolium* (Diamond Laurel) has broad, toothed, dark green leaves. Terminal clusters of white flowers over summer are followed by small but dramatic orange berries which remain on plants for a number of months. *P. undulatum* (Sweet Pittosporum) is a tall shrub or small tree. Although its cream flowers have a wonderful floral perfume during spring it can be a feral weed and is best not grown near bushland beyond its natural distribution.

Pomaderris

Plants of this genus are sadly, generally neglected. Many have ornamental foliage and the clusters of flowers, although not outstanding, are decorative and regularly visited by butterflies and other insects. Some are food plants for butterfly larvae. *Pomaderris aspera* (Hazel Pomaderris) may reach small tree proportions and is excellent for semi-shaded moist sites. It has broad, hairy leaves and clusters of cream flowers in spring. *P. ferruginea* (Rusty Pomaderris) and *P. lanigera* (Woolly Pomaderris) both have felty leaves and yellow flowers during spring.

Prostanthera
Mint-bushes

Mint-bushes are highly renowned for their fragrant foliage. Most are not generally regarded as plants which are attractive to wildlife but those species which have flattened tubular flowers are visited by honeyeaters, and insects are common on many of the white-flowered species of typical mint-bushes. The dwarf *Prostanthera aspalathoides* (Scarlet Mint-bush) needs maximum sunshine in a well-drained site to do well. Its flowers can be red, yellow or orange and are produced throughout the year with a peak in spring and summer. *P. monticola* (sometimes sold wrongly as *P. walteri*) is a spreading, low shrub with dark green leaves and pale bluish-green flowers during summer. *P. lasianthos* (Victorian Christmas Bush) is an excellent insect attractant. Shrubby and small tree selections are available with white, pink or mauve to purplish flowers over late spring and early summer.

A praying mantid ootheca (egg capsule) is attached to *Pultenaea gunnii*.

Pultenaea
Bush-peas

Bush-peas are excellent for attracting butterflies and their seeds are eaten by rosellas and bronze-wing pigeons. *Pultenaea juniperina* (Prickly Bush-pea) suckers and can form excellent thickets which small birds will use for nesting and as a refuge. The sweetly fragrant pea-flowers are produced in spring. *P. scabra* (Rough Bush-pea) does well in shady spots and the orange and yellow flowers are often profuse during spring. *P. gunnii* is short-lived, 4–5 years, but flowers heavily.

Rhodomyrtus trineura
Ironwood

This tropical species is a tall shrub to small tree which adapts to temperate regions. Although not highly ornamental it is valuable because its globular, cream fruits are devoured by birds. The small white to pink flowers bloom sporadically.

Schefflera actinophylla
Umbrella Tree

This tall shrub or small tree is one of the world's most popular indoor plants. A lover of warmth, it performs best in tropical and subtropical regions but can grow well in temperate zones if in a warm protected site. Large radiating spikes of small bright red, nectar-rich flowers are produced in spring and summer, and may extend into autumn. The fleshy black fruits are eagerly sought by birds and other animals.

Senecio
Fireweeds; Groundsels

Senecios are useful plants and even though they may quickly become leggy and are perhaps short-lived, they respond well to pruning which usually results in bushy plants. *Senecio linearifolius* (Firewood Groundsel) is stunning when its bright yellow daisies are in full bloom during late spring and summer. *S. lautus* (Variable Groundsel), which occurs from the coast to the alps, is a low, sometimes spreading shrub with bright green foliage and showy yellow daisies over spring and summer.

Solanum
Kangaroo Apples; Nightshades

These quick growing, small to tall shrubs are excellent because of their fruit production. *Solanum aviculare* (Kangaroo Apple) has entire or lobed dark green leaves and its violet to purple, spreading flowers are produced mainly in spring and summer. The elongated, small, tomato-like fruits are orange to brilliant red and non-poisonous when fully ripe. They contain many seeds which are enjoyed by birds. Green fruits are poisonous. The very closely allied *S. laciniatum* (Large Kangaroo Apple) has orange-yellow fruits.

Spyridium parvifolium
Australian Dusty Miller

The shrubby forms of this species differ only in their growth habit from the prostrate selection described on page 43. Upright forms can reach 3m tall by 2m across.

Syzygium wilsonii ssp. wilsonii
(syn. *Eugenia wilsonii*)

A spreading shrub of about 3m x 3m, which can be slow to establish. It is best suited to tropical and subtropical regions. Has magnificent red to burgundy flushes of new growth. The fluffy pink to scarlet heads of flowers are produced during winter to early summer and are followed by edible cream fruits.

Telopea
Waratahs

Waratahs are among the most spectacular of Australian plants and are highly regarded for attracting nectar-feeding birds. *Telopea speciosissima* (New South Wales Waratah) has large, usually brilliant red, flower-heads, but the cultivar 'Wirrimbirra White' has white flowers with tinges of pale yellowish green. Both flower in spring. There are a number of other cultivars becoming available. *T. oreades* (Gippsland Waratah) has flat-topped, red flower-heads and can be a small tree. *T. truncata* (Tasmanian Waratah) also has flattish, usually red flower-heads.

Telopea oreades

Templetonia retusa
Cockies' Tongues

A handsome, tall shrub with greyish-green to glaucous foliage. It is ideal for alkaline soils and coastal sites. It adapts to other conditions too. The pink to red pea-flowers are often profuse during winter and spring.

Thryptomene saxicola
Rock Thryptomene

A spreading, dwarf to small shrub with arching branches and small leaves. The long-lasting whitish, pale pink or deep pink flowers are borne during autumn to spring. Excellent for attracting butterflies such as the small Blues and other insects like hoverflies and small beetles. *T. denticulata* is also low-growing.

Thryptomene denticulata

Viminaria juncea
Native Broom

A quick-growing, fine-foliaged, medium to tall shrub with pendulous branchlets. During spring and early summer, the massed, lightly fragrant, yellow pea-flowers produce a captivating display. Pays to remove old or dead branches.

Westringia

All westringias are good for attracting insects. *Westringia fruticosa* (Coast Rosemary) is one of the most adaptable species. Its flowers are basically white with purple markings, blooming mainly during spring and summer. This is an excellent hedging plant. *W.* 'Wynyabbie Gem' has lilac flowers for most of the year and attractive greyish-green foliage. It also responds well to pruning. *W. glabra* (Violet Westringia) has mauve to violet flowers during spring and summer.

Wilkiea
Wilkieas

These are uncommon in cultivation but are valuable butterfly-attractants. *W. huegeliana* (Common Wilkiea) is a bushy, tall shrub with large, dark green toothed leaves. It produces clusters of small fragrant yellow flowers during summer and they are followed by small glossy black fruits. *W. macrophylla* (Large-leaved Wilkiea) grows taller. It has handsome, reddish, young growth and larger stiff leaves with prickly toothed margins. Butterflies may like the flowers but to the human nose their fragrance is somewhat off-putting. Best planted away from commonly used areas.

Zieria
Zierias

This genus is in the citrus family and is closely allied to *Boronia*. They are becoming more popular in cultivation after many years of neglect. A broad range of butterflies and many small insects such as hoverflies visit plants. *Zieria* 'Pink Crystals' is a small shrub which produces its small pink, starry flowers in spring, displayed against the greyish-green foliage. *Z. laevigata*, a parent of the above plant, has shiny, dark green leaves and during spring the white to pale pink flowers can be profuse.

Trees

Trees make more impact on the landscape than any other plant and they are tremendously important to birds and animals. Birds often use trees as lookouts. When eucalypts mature, their heartwood often decomposes to form hollows in the branches and trunks. It is in these hollows that a great number of native birds such as rosellas and other parrots, kookaburras and kingfishers, and animals such as possums and their relatives make their homes.

Trees placed in the right position will enhance any site. Conversely, they will cause much consternation if planted in the wrong spot, not only because of their unsuitability but also because you may incur considerable removal costs. It pays to consider thoroughly where you are going to plant trees!

Acacia
Wattles

The importance of wattles for wildlife habitat has become better understood in recent years, especially with regard to butterfly populations. *Acacia* flowers are very attractive to other insects which in turn are a staple food for many birds. Wattles usually provide a very attractive floral display and their seed production benefits many birds including rosellas and pigeons. The appendage to wattle seeds, called an aril, is a significant part of the diet of some ants. Another very important aspect of cultivating wattles is that their roots have nitrogen-fixing capabilities, which is beneficial for other plants.

Acacia floribunda (White Sallow Wattle) grows to about 4–8m x 4–8m. Its creamy yellow, rod-like flowerheads are produced during late winter and spring, and they are highly insect-attracting. Plants are usually bushy to near ground level.

Australia's floral emblem, *A. pycnantha* (Golden Wattle) does best in well-drained, sunny sites. Its golden flower-balls, during late winter and early spring, contrast well with the glossy, dark green leaves, which are somewhat like gum leaves.

A. dealbata (Silver Wattle) has delicate bluish- or greyish-green, ferny foliage which, when viewed from below, has a lacy appearance. The bright light yellow balls appear during late winter and early spring. It is quick growing and mature plants often have lovely lichens adorning the erect trunks. Plants may reach 6–30m x 5–10m.

Acmena ingens
(syn. *A. brachyandra*)
Red Apple

This fairly slow-growing tree of up to 15m tall has reddish, new leaves which become shiny, dark green and up to 17cm long. During late spring and early summer the small cream to white flowers are displayed in terminal heads. They are followed by edible, globular reddish fruits to about 4cm in diameter; fruit ripens during autumn to early spring. Suitable for subtropical and temperate areas. Appreciates slow release fertilisers and supplementary watering during dry periods. The allied *A. graveolens* (Large-fruited Satinash) can be taller and is best suited to large gardens in tropical and subtropical regions. It has larger, pear-shaped, red fruits.

Acronychia acidula
Lemon Aspen

A relatively slow-growing plant which becomes a medium-sized tree. It has thin, dark green leaves and during late spring to autumn produces fragrant spicy, small creamy-yellow flowers which are arranged in dense clusters. The decorative, white-ribbed fruit have a lovely citrus flavour and can be used for cordial-making. Best for tropical and subtropical regions. May need watering during extended dry periods.

Allocasuarina
(syn. *Casuarina*)
She-oaks

Most she-oaks have unusual and intriguing branchlets and some also have marvellous bark. The Rose She-oak or Forest Oak, *Allocasuarina torulosa*, can have deeply fissured, buff to deep brown fibrous bark. Some seedlings develop lovely burgundy to blackish foliage and plants with a pendulous habit are also particularly eye-catching.

A. littoralis (Black She-oak) has dark bark and upright branches with greenish branchlets. The reddish, fluffy, female flowers are on older wood while the brownish male flowers are in profuse narrow spikes at the ends of the branchlets. Both these trees usually grow 8–15m tall and flowering is mainly during autumn and winter.

Alphitonia excelsa
Red Ash; Soap Tree

This fast-growing tree has large elliptical leaves which are shiny dark green above and whitish below. During summer and autumn the small, fragrant greenish-white flowers are displayed in crowded clusters. The small, globular black fruits ripen during spring and summer. The closely allied Pink Ash or White Ash, *A. petrei*, has fragrant white flowers. Both of these small- to medium-sized trees are suited to growing in tropical, sub-tropical and temperate areas. They tolerate light frosts. Excellent for quickly providing foliage cover.

Angophora costata
Smooth-barked Apple

This must be one of Australia's best smooth-barked trees. During summer and autumn the mature greyish bark sheds in large patches to reveal lovely bright orange-brown to pink-brown bark. In late spring and summer the foliage may be completely covered by sweetly scented, cream flowers and clamorous insects and birds. Often this species has a contorted trunk and branches, which can be part of its attraction. All other angophoras have characteristics which make them valuable for wildlife habitat. The smaller *A. hispida* (Dwarf Apple) has heart-shaped greyish leaves.

Atherospermum moschatum
Southern Sassafras; Black Sassafras

This stately tree is a lover of moist, well-drained, semi-shaded to shaded sites. The combination of glossy, nutmeg-scented leaves and lovely fragrant, open-petalled white to cream flowers make it highly appealing to humans and insects alike. Plants are usually slow-growing but may reach 10–25m x 2–8m. Can be pruned or clipped.

Backhousia citriodora
Lemon-scented Myrtle

A highly desirable, small- to medium-sized tree with clusters of small cream flowers in summer and autumn. Plants tolerate sporadic, light frosts. They may need supplementary watering during dry periods. Never rake up dead leaves, or you will miss out on the superlative fragrance gained from crushing the leaves as you walk. *B. myrtifolia* (Ironwood) is not so fragrant but flowering plants during spring and summer are attractive to insects.

Banksia
Honeysuckles

Banksia integrifolia (Coast Banksia) are captivating on windy days as the leaves are ruffled to reveal their silvery undersides. During autumn to spring pale lemon-yellow bottlebrush-like spikes are produced. The allied *B. marginata* (Silver Banksia) is described on page 47.

B. serrata (Saw Banksia) is well known for its role in the tales of 'Snugglepot and Cuddlepie'. The large grey and greenish-yellow flower-cones are produced during late winter to autumn. It needs plenty of space in which to develop.

Beilschmiedia
Walnuts

These medium to tall trees are best in large gardens. They have a dense canopy of glossy foliage and highly perfumed, creamish flowers in large clusters during winter and spring. The small oval black fruits ripen in late winter and spring and are enjoyed by birds. The Bush Walnut or Hard Bollygum, *Beilsch-miedia obtusifolia* and *B. elliptica* (Grey Walnut) are worth trying and they tolerate irregular light frosts.

Brachychiton

The flamboyance of a Flame Tree, *Brachychiton acerifolius* in full flower during late spring and summer is always appreciated, but it can be some years before the splendid red tubular flowers come again. The bright green, lobed leaves form a dense shade-giving canopy. Similarly the Lacebark or White Kurrajong, *B. discolor* provides shade, except over the flowering season of summer and autumn, when the leaves can drop before the large dull pink to reddish flowers are displayed. These two trees are best suited to large gardens, but they respond well to pruning.

Brachychiton acerifolius

Callicoma serratifolia
Black Wattle

This is the small tree which early settlers used to build 'wattle-and-daub' huts. It is excellent for shady sites. The rusty-coloured, young shoots grow into olive-green toothed leaves. During spring and early summer the cream to pale yellow balls of flower attract butterflies and other insects. A very adaptable species which can vary in height from 4–10m.

Callistemon
Bottlebrushes

Quite a number have been described in 'Shrubs' on page 48. *Callistemon* 'Harkness' and selections of *C. viminalis* reach tree proportions after many years. Pink Tips or Willow Bottlebrush, *C. salignus* is a very reliable and attractive small tree. It has lovely brownish, papery bark, pink flushes of new foliage growth, and cream or sometimes pink, red or mauve brushes which are produced during spring to early summer. Although it appreciates moisture it does tolerate extended dry periods.

Other tall bottlebrushes to plant include River Bottlebrush, *C. sieberi* (previously known as *C. paludosus*) and *C. shiressii*.

Callitris
Cypress Pines

Australia has few conifers and most are in this genus. Parrots extract winged seeds from the woody cones produced by many species.

Callitris glaucophylla (White Cypress Pine) is a medium-sized tree with rough, greyish bark and greyish-green foliage. *C. rhomboidea* (Port Jackson Pine) is a tall shrub to small tree with greyish-green foliage.

Castanospermum australe
Black Bean; Moreton Bay Chestnut

Can develop into a stately tree and is therefore recommended for large gardens and parks. The glossy, dark leaves have many oblong leaflets and when plants are old enough the red and reddish yellow pea-flowers are produced during spring on bare branches. Fermentation of the nectar can occur and birds such as lorikeets may become intoxicated!

Ceratopetalum gummiferum
NSW Christmas Bush

Usually develops as a fairly erect small tree. During spring the small, white, starry flowers are produced and as they age the petals drop. Calyces enlarge and turn red, providing a wonderful sight during summer and early autumn. To obtain the best effect plants need plenty of sunshine.

Elaeocarpus reticulatus
Blueberry Ash

This adaptable, small evergreen tree has dark green foliage. Each old leaf turns red before it is shed. The delicately fringed, white or pink bell-like flowers are displayed during spring and early summer, followed by small, very dark blue berries. Other wildlife-attracting *Elaeocarpus* include *E. angustifolius* (syn. *E. grandis*) (Blue Quandong), another known also as Blueberry Ash, *E. obovatus*, and *E. bancroftii* (Ebony Heart). All are suitable for large gardens and parks.

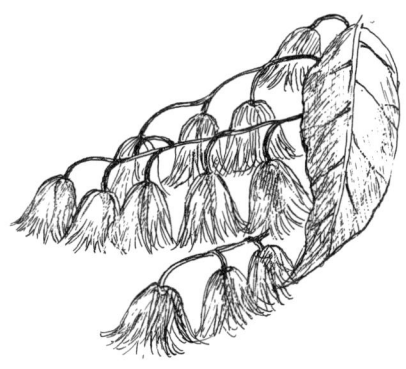

Elaeocarpus reticulatus

Eucalyptus
Eucalypts; Gums

Australia is the home of eucalypts and with over 700 species from which to choose there are trees for virtually every situation. All species have attributes which attract wildlife. Many species are prolific nectar-producers. Other eucalypts produce fruit which appeals to parrots. Gums provide nesting sites for larger birds such as magpies, ravens, currawongs, parrots, some owls and tawny frogmouths. Some aged eucalypts develop hollows in their branches and this is where parrots, kookaburras, kingfishers, some owls such as the Boobook, pardalotes, some ducks, bats and possum family members make their homes. The following selection of species gives you just an inkling of the possibilities.

Eucalyptus ficifolia (Scarlet Flowering Gum) is perhaps the best known of this genus. A splendid display of flowers during summer virtually covers the tree with any colour from pink, various shades of red, scarlet, orange, cream or white. Yellow Gum (called Blue Gum in some states), *E. leucoxylon* is renowned for its long flowering period during autumn to spring, when the cream to red flowers literally drip with nectar. Some of the low growing forms are very popular.

E. caesia is spectacular with its curling reddish brown bark, grey to glaucous young branches and bright pink, pendent flowers in winter and spring. This beautiful plant does best if left to grow *without* regular watering and fertilising. It needs to develop gradually because if it grows too quickly it can be unstabilised by excessive foliage. The large-flowered variant, known as ssp. *magna*, or 'Silver Princess' is usually more commonly available than the under-rated smaller-flowered member. It does not do well in tropical regions.

E. curtisii (Plunkett Mallee) is suited to tropical, subtropical and temperate regions. It has a greyish trunk with pendent branches and narrow leaves. During spring the heads of cream flowers can be spectacular. Further tropical species are *E. miniata* (Darwin Woollybutt) which produces a marvellous display of orange or scarlet flowers from autumn to spring and *E. ptychocarpa* (Swamp Bloodwood) which has white, pink, apricot or red flowers mainly in autumn to early spring.

For harsh coastal conditions *E. diversifolia* (Soap Mallee) is highly recommended. It has a floriferous display in late autumn and spring with a strong honey fragrance.

Many eucalypts have almost unnoticeable flowers but they can certainly offer foliages of different hues and fragrances. Silvery foliage plants are always popular and among the best and most reliable are *E. cinerea* (Argyle Apple), *E. cephalocarpa* (Mealy Stringybark) and *E. crenulata* (Victorian Silver Gum). Moths are attracted to these trees and moth caterpillars chew the foliage. Usually this does little harm; it is a natural method of pruning.

The Cadaga or Cadaghi, *E. torelliana* is from tropical north-eastern Queensland but it will grow as far south as Melbourne if given a warm to hot, protected site. The lower trunk is dark and rough and the upper part is smooth and green. The bright green leaves are very hairy when young and new growth may be reddish. White flowers which are produced during summer.

Some other species that are particularly attractive to wildlife are: *E. burdettiana*, *E. conferruminata*, *E. macrandra*, *E. megacornuta*, *E. sideroxylon* and *E. tricarpa*.

Euodia
Evodias

A member of the citrus family, the Pink-flowered Evodia or Corkwood, *Euodia elleryana* is prized because it is the host plant for caterpillars of the superb Ulysses Butterfly in tropical Queensland. The dark green, glossy leaves contrast vividly with the clusters of small nectar-rich flowers in summer and autumn. During spring and early summer there are shiny, dark seeds which attract birds. Responds well to watering and fertilising. The allied *E. bonwickiana* (Yellow Evodia) provides shade with its dense canopy. It has pink to reddish flowers in autumn.

Ficus
Figs

Most Australian figs develop into sizeable trees and are therefore best planted in large gardens or parks — they are notorious for blocking drains with their roots. Figs are prolific producers of fruits which are avidly eaten by birds and animals. *Ficus benjamina* (Weeping Fig) forms a dense canopy and has deep to bright red fruits which ripen during spring to summer. The Port Jackson Fig or Rusty Fig, *F. rubiginosa* is also popular with its broad, deep green leaves. Warty yellow to deep red fruits ripen from late summer to spring. *F. coronata* (Creek Sandpaper Fig) has intriguing rough leaves and hairy, black fruits which mature during late summer to early winter. Other excellent figs are *F. microcarpa*, *F. obliqua*, *F. hispida* and *F. platypoda*.

Flindersia australis
Crow's Ash

This member of the citrus family is an excellent medium tree with smooth grey bark and broad leaves with glossy green leaflets. The small, white to cream flowers are not highly ornamental but many insects find them very attractive. The decorative prickly fruits open like a starfish when fully ripe to release the seeds.

Grevillea
Grevilleas; Silky Oaks

Some of the tall grevilleas are spectacular trees when in flower. Their flowers produce a long-lasting nectar flow and many of the fruits are an important food for animals. Most gardeners would be familiar with the orange flowers in summer of *G. robusta* (Silky Oak). It is an adaptable tree which will grow well in tropical to temperate regions. *Grevillea baileyana* (Findlay's Silky Oak) does best in tropical and subtropical regions. The stunning rusty or golden-brown undersurfaces of the leaves contrast vividly with the dark green upper surface, especially on windy days. It has sweetly-scented, creamy flowers in summer.

Harpullia pendula
Tulipwood

This is an excellent shade-providing small to medium tree with pale green pinnate leaves. The faintly fragrant, greenish flowers are borne in open panicles during summer and splendid yellowish to reddish fruits ripen and split open in spring to reveal glossy, dark brown to black seeds.

Hymenosporum flavum
Native Frangipani

A tree with wonderfully fragrant, cream to yellow flowers during late spring to early summer, which gain purplish tonings as they mature. Some trees may have sparse foliage but they respond well to medium or hard pruning. Every garden should have at least one *Hymenosporum flavum*!

Melaleuca
Paperbarks; Honey-myrtles

Most of the tall melaleucas have thick, papery bark which is often ornamental but can also be functional when it protects the trunk from fire. Many birds find the bark an excellent nest-making material.

Melaleuca argentea (Silver-leaved Paperbark) often has a spreading canopy and cream to greenish flower-brushes during winter to spring. *M. decora* has dark green, narrow leaves and sweetly-scented, white to cream brushes in late spring and summer. The Swamp Paperbark or Needle-leaved Honey-myrtle, *M. rhaphiophylla* is well-liked by many for its greyish to brownish papery bark and pendulous branchlets. White to pale yellowish-green flowers bloom during summer to early winter. *M. quinquenervia* (Broad-leaved Paperbark) is a very adaptable species which produces its white, cream or rarely red brushes mainly during spring and summer.

Melia azedarach
White Cedar

A handsome, umbrageous tree with glossy, divided leaves and profuse clusters of small, sweetly scented flowers of lilac with dark brown and white during late spring and early summer. Usually deciduous in late winter or early spring. Highly recommended for low rainfall areas (may need supplementary watering until well established).

Neolitsea dealbata
Hard-leaved Bolly Gum

Usually develops into a bushy, small tree and has attractive, fairly large oval leaves. The small yellowish flowers are unisexual and bloom in autumn to early winter. You will need at least one female tree and one male tree to have plants bearing the egg-shaped, purplish black fruit. Plants dislike strong hot winds.

Podocarpus elatus
Brown Pine

This appealing, small to medium, spreading tree has scaly, brown bark and long, narrow, glossy dark green leaves. Minute unisexual flowers are on separate trees. Fruiting is during late summer and winter; the fleshy, turpentine-flavoured, blackish-blue fruit-stalk is favoured by birds.

Polyscias

Polyscias elegans (Celery Wood) is a fast-growing small to medium tree which develops a shady canopy. The long, frond-like leaves have many dark green leaflets. During late summer and autumn large panicles of small purplish flowers are produced, followed fairly quickly by small, round, fleshy black fruits which are eagerly devoured by birds.
P. sambucifolius (Elderberry Panax) may be a tall shrub or small tree which can sucker and form a copse. The small creamish flowers are followed by translucent fruits.

Stenocarpus sinuatus
Firewheel Tree

A magnificent tree once it reaches the flowering stage — this can take 7–15 years. It has glossy, deep green, deeply lobed leaves and outstanding bright red flowers. Flowering starts in late summer and can continue until early spring. Plants flower best in a sunny site. The Red Silky Oak or Scrub Beefwood, *S. salignus* attracts insects to its small, sweetly-scented white flowers.

Stenocarpus salignus

Syzygium
Lilly Pillies; Brush Cherries

The value of lilly pillies for wildlife can never be overstated as they can be prodigious producers of edible fruits, although some plants may go for a few years producing little or no fruit. The flowers are rich in nectar for birds and insects. Densely foliaged plants are often used for nesting sites.

The Scrub Cherry or Creek Cherry, *Syzygium australe* is a densely foliaged, small to medium tree with dark green leaves. Small white flowers are displayed in fluffy clusters during summer and early autumn and are followed by tasty, pink to purplish red fruits. *S. fibrosum* (Fibrous Satinash) is a small tree with lovely purplish young growth that later becomes glossy dark green. The dull orange to brownish flowers usually appear between mid-autumn and early summer and are followed by sizeable, bright red, fleshy fruits. Cherry Satinash or Small-leaved Water Gum, *S. luehmannii* can have delicately coloured, pale pink young growth. Its white flowers bloom in spring and early summer and the oblong, bright pinkish-red fruits, ripening during late spring and early autumn, have a luminescent quality.

Other species worth growing are
S. paniculatum (Magenta Cherry),
S. crebrinerve (Rose Satinash)
S. francisii (Giant Water Gum), also known as Rose Satinash and
S. oleosum (Blue Cherry or Blue Lilly Pilly). Most of the syzygiums respond very well to pruning and clipping.

Tristaniopsis laurina
(syn. *Tristania laurina*)
Water Gum; Kanuka

The charm of this tree grows as it develops its framework of smooth, pale-barked trunks. The leaves are glossy and dark green. In summer and early autumn clusters of small, deep yellow flowers are displayed. Many members of the parrot family eat the fruit seeds.

Tristaniopsis laurina

Xanthostemon chrysanthus
Golden Penda

A handsome, small tree with lovely reddish young growth followed by large glossy dark green leaves. In autumn it produces crowded heads of golden-yellow flowers. Excellent for subtropical regions. The allied x *oppositifolius* is a medium-sized tree that has greenish-white flowers during late autumn to early spring. Not recommended for small gardens.

Introduced Predators

The natural environment in Australia, which has evolved in isolation for millions of years, is now home to some major predatory introduced species. These intruders have had a significant effect on the wildlife population. Three of the most serious offenders are cats, dogs and foxes. Australian animals have not had sufficient time to develop a self-protective fear of these predators.

A continuing, integrated control of these animals, many of which have become feral, is needed. A balanced approach is required: reducing the population of only one predator, say the fox, may simply allow another animal population to increase, in this instance, feral cats.

Cats

Cats can be lovely responsive animals that thrive on the attention of humans, but most of these sweetly purring pussies are also extremely proficient hunters. Recent studies in Victoria show that an estimated 211 million wild animals and birds are killed by that state's estimated 1.4 million pet, stray and feral cats. It is not the cat's fault. It is we humans who have not managed and maintained our cats properly and humanely.

One of the main contributors to these statistics is our lethargy in knowing the whereabouts of our cats. In Victoria alone it is estimated that the 900,000 pet cats may kill 29 million birds and animals each year. A staggering statistic: even if they kill only one tenth of that number it is far too many!

Free-roaming stray cats, as well as true feral cats, are the major contributors to wildlife fatalities. Recent studies by Dr D. A. Paton of Adelaide University on cat dietary habits have shown that cats can kill and eat an average of more than 100 native birds; 50 small mammals; 50 reptiles; 3 frogs; and various other smaller animals over a period of one year. Another problem is that native animals have no resistance to certain blood diseases and bacteria spread by cats.

It is possible to enjoy the companionship of cats if you adhere to some rigid guidelines. Cats must not be let roam at will. Confinement can be beneficial to cats in the long term. Research has shown that the average age of domestic cats confined to living indoors in 12 years, while domestic cats which are left to free-range have an average lifespan of about 3 years.

Confinement covers a number of options. Cats may be kept within the house at all times, provided all their needs are met. A cat must be free to exercise at will, but it also needs 19 hours of sleep per day. They can have direct access from indoors to specially designed cattery areas which allow plenty of movement. Some cat lovers have constructed special runways

---

It is a myth that well-fed cats do not attack wildlife. There is also quite substantial evidence that cats with bells around their necks are also wildlife killers. Cats, in fact, learn that bells can warn wildlife and endeavour to make sure their movements do not ring their bell.

which connect the house and cattery enclosure. If you would like further details on cattery design you can contact your local Royal Society for the Prevention of Cruelty to Animals office, or veterinarian for advice.

All cats should have an identification tag so the owner can be notified as soon as possible if the animal strays or is injured. And a warning: recent legislation in New South Wales classes cats as noxious animals if they roam more than one kilometre from a house — it then becomes legal for the cat to be killed.

Dogs

There is a well-worn cliché about a dog being your best friend, however, there can be some negative aspects to having dogs as pets if we fail to provide facilities for its enjoyment within the boundaries of our own properties. Many domestic dogs, as well as stray and feral dogs, are responsible for the reduction of our wildlife population.

Much of the damage to wildlife from domestic dogs would not occur if owners took proper action to restrict the movement of these animals beyond their boundaries, especially if bushland is nearby. Dogs can have a roaming range of about thirty kilometres per night and during the period from dusk to dawn they can severely disrupt the activities of much of our nocturnal native wildlife.

Small mammals and reptiles are among the dog's most common victims and they may end up on your back doorstep. If owners are responsible for their dog's activities and aware of the consequences of letting dogs wander, there is no reason why a dog should be a threat to our wildlife.

Foxes

The European Red Fox, *Vulpes vulpes* was introduced into Australia, near Melbourne, during the mid to late 19th-century for sporting purposes. By 1917 foxes were recorded in Kalgoorlie, Western Australia. Currently they are known to occur in more than two-thirds of our continent, ranging from rainforest to semi-arid regions.

Over fifty species of native animals are known to be part of the fox's diet, and it is also a successful predator of brolga chicks and other young birds which are nestlings at near ground level. Six mammal species have become extinct in the Victorian Mallee, and the fox was the main predator of these mammals. Foxes attack platypuses and also, in summer, excavate and consume tortoise eggs. Blackberries, a noxious weed, are an important food source for foxes in late summer and autumn, and so foxes act as a major dispersal agent of seeds, which germinate freely. Foxes are also known carriers of diseases which affect our wildlife and domestic animals. There is extreme concern that foxes may become carriers of rabies if that disease ever enters Australia.

Foxes are very agile creatures and the tall fences of suburbia do not keep them out. They can also climb to the lower branches of trees. Effective fox control programmes can be implemented. Baits developed specifically for fox control are available: they are sometimes marketed under the name 'Foxoff'. Further details are available from government conservation departments or private consultants.

Did you know that cats can be readily trained to walk with a cat lead or harness? Take your cat for a stroll around your garden or around the block!

If you don't wish to breed it is recommended that domestic cats be desexed, for a number of reasons:
- they usually make better pets
- they are easier to care for
- they are less inclined to territorial activities
- there is less stress placed upon them by breeding activities
- it restricts the possibility of having unwanted litters

The addresses of nature conservation agencies are:

ACT:
Australian Capital Territory Parks and Conservation Service
PO Box 1119,
Tuggeranong, ACT, 2909
Phone (06) 207 1143
Fax (06) 207 2229

NT:
Conservation Commission of the Northern Territory
PO Box 496,
Palmerston, NT, 0831
Phone (089) 89 4542
Fax (089) 89 4510

NSW:
NSW National Parks and Wildlife Service
PO Box 1967,
Hurstville, NSW, 2220
Phone (02) 585 6444
Fax (02) 585 6555

SA:
South Australian National Parks and Wildlife Service
PO Box 1782, Adelaide, SA, 5001
Phone (08) 207 2000
Fax (08) 207 2235

VIC:
Land for Wildlife
PO Box 137
Heidelberg, VIC, 3084
Phone (03) 450 8600
Fax (03) 450 8737

TAS:
Parks and Wildlife Service
Department of Environment and Land Management
GPO Box 44A
Hobart, TAS, 7001
Phone (002) 33 8011
Fax (002) 24 0884

WA:
Western Australian Dept. of Conservation and Land Management
PO Box 104, Como, WA, 6152,
Phone (09) 367 0333
Fax (09) 367 0475

Land for Wildlife

Land for Wildlife is a wonderful scheme which enables landholders of any category, i.e. farmers, municipalities, community groups, schools and home-owners, to voluntarily participate in wildlife conservation, provided that the qualification standards, as set down by *Land for Wildlife* are met by applicants. Emphasis is on registering country and rural properties with significant habitat potential. Suburban sites are considered for registration if a group of like-minded neighbours are willing to be participants in the scheme and if their land can jointly provide significant wildlife habitat. There are now over 2200 registered properties in Victoria alone giving a total of some 39 000 hectares of wildlife habitat. Hundreds more properties are awaiting registration.

The scheme in Victoria is administered by the Department of Conservation and Natural Resources with the assistance of the Bird Observers' Club of Australia, an entirely voluntary community organisation. The depletion of bushland over the years since white settlement has been dramatic and *Land for Wildlife* is a major contributor in trying to reverse that situation on private land, which accounts for two-thirds of the State's area.

The main aim of *Land for Wildlife* is to encourage and assist landholders to provide suitable habitat for wildlife on their properties, thus providing the opportunity for wildlife numbers to increase. Advice is given on how to integrate wildlife habitats with other uses of the property.

Registered *Land for Wildlife* participants who feel that they need assistance in management of wildlife habitat can readily gain information and practical advice. The local *Land for Wildlife* extension officers are able and experienced people and if they cannot provide relevant assistance they will put you in touch with people who can help. There are also field days and social activities which are always worth attending. They provide an excellent opportunity to discuss successes and you may also find answers to some of your habitat management problems.

Participants receive the *Land for Wildlife* notes and newsletter and I can thoroughly recommend this material as a marvellous resource covering all aspects of wildlife. The sign supplied by the scheme enables you to advertise your commitment to nature conservation which is achieved in unison with other property uses.

Further reading

Plants

Australian Plant Study Group, *Grow What* Series, Thomas Nelson, Melbourne, 1980–85
Elliot, G. M., *The Gardener's Guide to Australian Plants*, Hyland House, Melbourne, 1985
Elliot, G. M., *The New Australian Plants for Small Gardens and Containers*, Hyland House, Melbourne, 1988
Elliot, W. R., & Jones, D. L. *Encyclopaedia of Australian Plants Suitable for Cultivation*, Volumes 1–6, Lothian, Melbourne, 1980–93
Jones, D. L., *Encyclopaedia of Ferns*, Lothian, Melbourne, 1987
Jones, D. L., *Palms in Australia*, Reed Books, Frenchs Forest, 1984
Jones, D. L., & Gray, B., *Climbing Plants in Australia*, Reed Books, Frenchs Forest NSW, 1988
Lord, E. E., & Willis, J. H., *Shrubs and Trees for Australian Gardens*, 5th edition, Lothian, Melbourne, 1982
Romanowski, N., *Water and Wetland Plants for Southern Australia*, Lothian, Melbourne, 1992
Wrigley, J. W. & Fagg, M., *Bird Attracting Plants*, Angus & Robertson, Sydney, 1990

Animals, birds and insects

Clyne, D., *The Garden Jungle*, Collins, Sydney, 1979
Clyne, D., *Wildlife in the Suburbs*, Oxford University Press, Melbourne, 1990
Coupar, P. & M., *Flying Colours, Common Caterpillars, Butterflies and Moths of South-eastern Australia*, New South Wales University Press, 1993
Hawkeswood, T. J., *Beetles of Australia*, Angus & Robertson, Sydney, 1987
Hero, J., Littlejohn, M. & Marantelli, G., *Frogwatch, Field Guide to Victorian Frogs*, Department of Conservation and Environment, Victoria Melbourne, 1991
Hockings, F. D., *Friends and Foes of Australian Gardens*, A.H. & A.W. Reed, Sydney, 1980
Hyett, J. & Shaw, N., *Australian Mammals, A Field Guide for New South Wales, Victoria, South Australia and Tasmania*, Nelson, Melbourne, 1980
Johnston, P. & Don, A., *Grow Your Own Wildlife*, Greening Australia Ltd, Canberra, 1990
McCulloch, E. M., *Your Garden Birds*, Hyland House, Melbourne, 1987
New, T. R., *Butterfly Conservation*, Entomological Society of Victoria, Melbourne, 1987
Pizzey, G., *A Field Guide to the Birds of Australia*, Collins, Sydney, 1980
Pizzey, G., *A Garden of Birds*, Viking O'Neil, Melbourne, 1988
Ride, W. D. L., *A Guide to the Native Animals of Australia*, Oxford University Press, Melbourne, 1970
Robinson, M., *A Field Guide to Frogs of Australia*, Australian Museum and Reed, Sydney, 1993
Simpson, K. & Day, N. *The Birds of Australia*, Lloyd O'Neil, South Yarra, 1984
Society for Growing Australian Plants, Tablelands Branch, *Attracting Butterflies to Your Garden*, Tolga, Queensland, 1987
Swanson, S., *Lizards of Australia*, Angus & Robertson, Sydney, 1976
Temby, I., *A Guide to Living with Wildlife*, Department of Conservation and Environment, Victoria, Melbourne, 1992
Wilson, J., (Ed.) *Victorian Urban Wildlife*, Angus & Robertson, Sydney, 1991

Garden design and construction

Adams, G. M., *Birdscaping Your Garden*, Rigby, Adelaide, 1980
Green, M., *Building the the Garden*, Lothian, Melbourne, 1980
Hutchison, F., *Creating a Native Garden for Birds*, Simon & Schuster, Sydney, 1990
Lochhead, H., *Gardens for Living*, Greenhouse, Richmond, Victoria, 1987
Molyneux, B., & Macdonald, R., *Native Gardens*, Thomas Nelson, Melbourne, 1983
Reader's Digest, *Practical Guide to Home Landscaping*, Reader's Digest, Surry Hills, NSW, 1973
Thompson, P., *Water in Your Garden*, Lothian, Melbourne, 1991
Wilson, G., *Landscaping with Australian Plants*, Thomas Nelson, Melbourne, 1975

Garden maintenance

Bradley, J., *Bringing Back the Bush*, Lansdowne, Sydney, 1988
C.S.I.R.O., *Discovering Soils Series*, CSIRO Division of Soils, Melbourne
Elliot, R., *Pruning, A Practical Guide*, 2nd. Ed. Lothian, Melbourne, 1993
Jones, D. L., & Elliot, W. R., *Pests, Diseases & Ailments of Australian Plants*, Lothian, Melbourne, 1986
Lamp, C., & Collet, F., *A Field Guide to Weeds in Australia*, Inkata Melbourne, 1988

Index

NOTE: Plant names listed in the grey panels throughout this book are not included in this index.

Acacia species 41, 46, 55
Acmena species 55
Acronychia acidula 55
Actinotus helianthi 37
Alectryon species 47
Alocasia macrorrhizos 38
Allocasuarina species 55
Alphitonia species 55
Angophora species 56
Anigozanthos species 56
Apple-berries 44
Archontophoenix 46
Atherospermum moschatum 56
Austromyrtus dulcis 47

Backhousia species 56
Baeckea species 47
Banksia species 47, 56
Bauera rubioides 41
Baumea articulata 38
Beach Cherry 49
Beilschmiedia species 56
Billardiera species 44
Billy Buttons 39
bird puddings 13
Bird's Eye 47
Black Bean 57
Blandfordia species 38
Blechnum species 45
Blueberry Ash 57
Bolwarra 49
Boobiallas 43, 52
Bottlebrushes 48, 56
Brachychiton species 56
Brachyscome multifida 41
Bracteantha bracteata 37
Breynia species 47
Broom, Native 54
Brown Pine 59
Brush Cherries 59
Buckinghamia celsissima 47
Bursaria spinosa 47
Bush-peas 53

Callicarpa pedunculata 48
Callicoma serratifolia 56
Callistemon species 48, 56
Callitris species 57
Calocephalus brownii 42
Calothamnus species 48
Calytrix species 48
Carex fascicularis 38
Carpentaria Palm 46
Cassia species 48
Castanospermum australe 57
Casuarina species 55
Ceratopetalum gummiferum 57
Chamelaucium species 48
Chionochloa pallida 38
Chorizema species 48
Christmas Bells 38
    Bush, NSW 57
Chrysocephalum species 41
Cissus antarctica 44
Clematis species 44
Cockies' Tongues 54
Coffee Bush 47
Common Correa 41
    Everlasting 41
Copper Laurel 49
Coral Peas 42
Cordyline species 49
Correa species 41, 49
Craspedia species 39
Crassula helmsii 41
Crinum species 39
Crow's Ash 58

Cunjevoi 38
Cushion Bush 42
Cut-leaf Daisy 41
Cyathea species 45
Cypress Pines 57

Daisy-bushes 52
Dianella species 39
Dicksonia antarctica 45
Dodonaea species 49
Dogwood 51
Doodia species 45
Doryanthes species 39
Drumsticks 39
Dusty Miller, Australian 43, 54

Eel Grass 40
Einadia nutans 41
Elaeocarpus species 57
Emu Bushes 41, 49
Epacris species 49
Eremophila species 41, 49
Eriostemon myoporoides 49
Eucalyptus species 57
Eugenia reinwardtiana 49
Euodia species 58
Eupomatia laurina 49
Everlastings 37, 38

Fan-flowers 43
Ferns 45
Ficus species 58
Figs 58
Finger Lime 52
Fireweeds 53
Firewheel Tree 59
Flame Peas 48
Flannel Flower 37
Flindersia australis 58
Fringe Myrtles 48

Gahnia species 39
Gleichenia species 45
Golden Penda 59
Goodenia ovata 49
Goodia lotifolia 50
Grevillea species 42, 50, 58
Groundsels 53
Guinea Flowers 42, 44
Gums 57

Hakea species 50
Hard-leaved Bolly Gum 58
Hardenbergia species 44
Harpullia pendula 58
Heaths 49
Helichrysum species 37, 41
Helipterum species 38
Hibbertia species 42, 44
Honey-myrtles 51, 58
Hop Bushes 49
    Goodenia 49
Hymenanthera dentata 51
Hymenosporum flavum 58
Hypocalymma species 51

Ironwood 53
Isolepis species 39
Isotoma 42
Ivory Curl 47

Jacksonia scoparia 51
Jasminum suavissimum 42
Jointed Twig Rush 38
Juncus species 39

Kangaroo Apples 53
    Grass 38
    Paws 38
Kanuka 59
Kennedia species 42

Koala food plants 30
Kunzea species 51

Lemon Aspen 55
Lemon-scented Myrtle 56
Leptospermum species 51
Leucophyta brownii 42
Lilies 38, 39, 40, 43, 49
Lilly Pillies 59
Linospadix monostachya 46
Lomandra species 39
Lomatia species 51
Long-leaved Waxflower 49

Marsh Flowers 40
Marshworts 43
Marsilea species 42
Matted Bush-pea 43
Melaleuca species 51, 58
Melia azedarach 58
Mentha species 42
Microcitrus australasica 52
Microlaena stipoides 38
Midgen Berry 47
Mint-bushes 53
Mints, Native 42
Mirbelia oxylobioides 52
Moreton Bay Chestnut 57
Morinda jasminoides 43
Morning Flags and Iris 39
Myoporum species 43, 52
Myriophyllum species 43

Nardoo 42
Native Frangipani 58
nectar feeders and mixture 12
Neolitsea dealbata 58
nesting sites and boxes 15–16
Net-bushes 48
Nodding Blue-lily 40
    Saltbush 41
Nymphoides species 43

Olearia species 52
Orthrosanthus species 39
Ottelia ovalifolia 43
Ovens Wattle 41

Palms 46
Paper Daisies 37
Paperbarks 51, 58
Parsonsia brownii 45
Passiflora species 45
Patersonia species 39
Phebalium species 49
Pimelea species 43, 52
Pittosporum species 52
Poa species 40
Podocarpus elatus 59
Polyscias species 59
Pomaderris species 53
Pratia pedunculata 43
Prostanthera species 53
Pultenaea species 43, 53
Purple Flags 39

Quince, Native 47

Rambutan, Smooth 47
Rasp Ferns 45
Red Ash 55
    Apple 55
Red-anther Wallaby Grass 38
Red-fruited Sword-sedge 39
Restio tetraphyllus 40
Rhagodia nutans 41
Rhodanthe species 38
Rhodomyrtus trineura 53
Ribbon Weed 40
Rice Flowers 43, 52
Rosemary, Coast 54

Rottnest Daisy 38
Running Postman 42
Rushes 39

Saltbushes 41
Sassafras 56
Satinwoods 52
Scaevola species 43
Schefflera actinophylla 53
seed trays and tables 13
Senecio species 53
She-oaks 55
Silky Oaks 58
Soap Tree 55
Solanum species 53
Southern Cross 44
Spoon Lily 38
Spyridium parvifolium 43, 54
Stenocarpus species 59
Sticherus species 45
Straw Flowers 37
Stylidium graminifolium 40
Stypandra species 40
Sunrays 38
Swamp Lily 39, 43
    Stonecrop 41
Sweet Jasmine 42
    Morinda 43
Syzygium species 54, 59

Tassel Sedge 38
Tassel-cord Rush 40
Tea-trees 51
Telopea species 54
Templetonia retusa 54
Thelionema caespitosum 40
Themeda triandra 38
Thryptomene species 54
Todea barbara 45
Trachymene coerulea 38
Tree Ferns 45
Trigger Plants 40
Triglochin species 40
Tristania laurina 54
Tristaniopsis laurina 59
Tufted Blue-lily 40
Tulipwood 58
Tussock Grasses 40
Twining Silkpod 45

Umbrella Tree 53

Vallisneria spiralis 40
Velvet Leaf 48
Villarsia species 40
Viminaria juncea 54
Viola hederacea 44
Violets, Australian 44, 51
    Tree 51

Walking Stick Palm 46
Walnuts 56
Waratahs 54
Water Ferns 45
    Gum 59
    Milfoils 43
    Ribbons 40
water-loving plants 7, 46
Watervine 44
Wattles, 41, 46, 55
Waxflowers 48
Weeping Grass 38
Westringia species 54
White Cedar 58
Wilkiea species 54
Wiry Bauera 41

Xanthosia rotundifolia 44
Xanthostemon species 59

Zieria species 54